*Storying Violence:*
*Unravelling Colonial Narratives*
*in the Stanley Trial*

# STORYING VIOLENCE

## UNRAVELLING COLONIAL NARRATIVES IN THE STANLEY TRIAL

Gina Starblanket & Dallas Hunt

with foreword by Tasha Hubbard and Jade Tootoosis

ARP BOOKS • WINNIPEG

ARP Books (Arbeiter Ring Publishing)
205-70 Arthur Street
Winnipeg, Manitoba
Treaty 1 Territory and Historic Métis Nation Homeland
Canada R3B 1G7
arpbooks.org

Book design and layout by Mike Carroll.
Cover artwork *Our Mother which art the Land* by Katherine Boyer.
Printed and bound in Canada by Imprimerie Gauvin on paper made
from 100% recycled post-consumer waste.

**Canada Council Conseil des Arts**
**for the Arts du Canada**

Canadä  Manitoba 🐃

ARP Books acknowledges the generous support of the Manitoba Arts Council and the Canada
Council for the Arts for our publishing program. We acknowledge the financial support of the
Government of Canada and the Province of Manitoba through the Book Publishing Tax Credit
and the Book Publisher Marketing Assistance Program of Manitoba Culture, Heritage, and
Tourism.

LIBRARY AND ARCHIVES CANADA CATALOGUING IN PUBLICATION

Title: Storying violence : unravelling colonial narratives in the Stanley trial / Gina Starblanket
    & Dallas Hunt ; with foreword by Tasha Hubbard and Jade Tootoosis.

Names: Starblanket, Gina, author. | Hunt, Dallas, 1987- author. | Hubbard, Tasha, writer of
    foreword. | Tootoosis, Jade, writer of foreword.

Identifiers: Canadiana (print) 20200258613 | Canadiana (ebook) 20200259946 | ISBN
9781927886373 (softcover) | ISBN 9781927886380 (ebook)

Subjects: LCSH: Stanley, Gerald (Farmer)—Trials, litigation, etc. | LCSH: Boushie, Colten.
| LCSH: Trials (Murder)—Saskatchewan. | LCSH: Trials (Manslaughter)—Saskatchewan.
| LCSH: Indigenous peoples—Saskatchewan. | LCSH: Saskatchewan—Race rela-
tions. | LCSH: Saskatchewan—Ethnic relations. | LCSH: Indigenous peoples—Violence
against—Saskatchewan.

Classification: LCC HV6535.C32 S29 2020 | DDC 364.152/3097124—dc23

# Contents

# ACKNOWLEDGMENTS

The authors would like to acknowledge with gratitude the Boushie and Baptiste families for their incredible patience, encouragement, and support in the composition of this book. We especially want to thank Jade Tootoosis and Tasha Hubbard for many important conversations that informed the writing of this project—it would not exist without the incisive insights they shared over the course of many generative discussions.

We acknowledge and recognize the contributions shared by those who participated in a 2018 Native American and Indigenous Studies Association (NAISA) roundtable on the topics taken up in this book, including Mylan Tootoosis, Erica Violet Lee, and Robert Innes. Profuse thanks to Heidi Kiiwetinepinesiik

Stark, Daniel Voth, Corey Snelgrove, and Sharon Stein for their thoughtful suggestions and important comments on the manuscript. Finally, many thanks to Todd Besant and Irene Bindi, and Bret Parenteau at ARP Books for their editorial oversight and constant encouragement at all stages of this project. We also extend our gratitude to Katherine Boyer for letting us use her beadwork *Our Mother, which art the Land* for the cover image.

Thanks especially to Debbie Baptiste, who has shown unwavering strength and fortitude in the face of systemic colonial injustice. We are in awe of her resolute courage. Kinanâskomitin, Debbie.

Finally, this book is dedicated to Colten Boushie and to all the Indigenous youth who have faced, and *continue* to face, virulent racism and violence in the prairies (and beyond).

*Tasha Hubbard & Jade Tootoosis*

W̶hen the family of the late Colten Boushie attend screenings of the feature documentary *nîpawis-tamâsowin: We Will Stand Up*, they have a special message to specific audience members; Colten's mother Debbie Baptiste tells the parents in the room to love, hug, and forgive their children, thus showing her capacity to focus on children's futures. Colten's sister and cousin Jade Tootoosis tells all the youth in the audience how much they are loved and valued. To the Indigenous youth, she tells them to not believe what is written in the media comments. Their message is to look to their families, communities and elders to find the strength to be themselves.

All the efforts made by the family in its advocacy work, and all the efforts that the filmmaking team of *nîpawistamâsowin* made, were done with the love we all have for the future genera-tions. The title of the film means that a strong, small group has the courage to stand up for what is right on behalf of a larger group. This is the spirit of the work the family continues to do.

We want Indigenous youth in North America to be free to create their own story: one that is filled with love, determination and pride. We envision a time in which we, as Indigenous people, are safe to be ourselves within our own lands. This is what we want for our youth and future generations.

Although some may have not known Colten personally, many supportive people felt compelled to reach out and share their condolences and concerns. Their compassion and empathy for the loss of life and the pain of the family instills a sense of hope in humanity. But many others have decided to sit behind their keyboards and write terrible and violent comments that aren't based on knowledge, awareness, or kindness, but rather on stereotypes, assumptions, and hate.

If Colten were here reading those comments, it would hurt him, because he was sensitive and caring. Indigenous people sadly have to learn to cope with online racism, and one strategy we have is to find humour, even in dark places. Colten would try to disguise his discomfort and hurt by trying to make light of it through a joke. But the family is here to hear those comments and it affects them deeply.

And now our young people read those comments.

Young Indigenous people living in what is currently called North America identify with Colten. They often experience the same judgements that some attempted to place on him. A colonial story was told by Stanley's defence, by online commentators, and the media: that somehow Colten deserved what happened to him. This connects to the mechanisms of colonialism that tell us we are not smart, we are not valued, we are less than.

Jade recalls how at the bail hearing, our family sat on one side and the Stanley family sat on the other. When the judge stood up to leave, the guards came in and stood between us, facing our family and supporters, as though we demonstrated the threat, despite the fact that our family were the victims.

After this first experience in the courthouse, the family felt as though Stanley was seen as a human being, even smiling at the jury during his testimony at the trial. But it felt like throughout the entire proceedings, despite being the victim, Colten was not allowed to be seen as a human being. Another element to the colonial story is the myth that Indigenous people are inherently dangerous. This is the sentiment that fueled the mass hanging of Cree men in 1885, who were executed without being allowed to have access to legal representation. This is why Tasha included this history in the film, to make the connection to the way patterns were set in the past and continue to be repeated to today.

Colonial stories thrive on Indigenous people's silence. And thus, the legal system that tried the case seemed to want Colten's family to remain silent, and the family refused to do so. They insisted on meetings when they weren't being informed of the proceedings. In one meeting, Jade remembers telling the prosecutors that she wanted them to understand that Colten was loved and meant the world to his family, and that it was hard when they didn't tell them anything. She told them that, as a family, they didn't ask for this situation, and they don't know how a murder trial works, and that it is hard when they don't know what is going on and they have to continually ask questions. When Jade became emotional, the assistant prosecutor accused her of yelling at them, which made the family concerned that the prosecutors were going to walk out of the meeting.

Throughout the process, the family had to balance their concerns and their fear that if they spoke up too much, or challenged too much, there would be repercussions. Now that the Saskatchewan legal system has denied an appeal, they no longer worry about speaking out on behalf of their loved one and for other victims of violence.

The Canadian legal system operates on the precedents of stories and decisions of earlier cases. And since the system was established through colonialism, many of the stories told are those which criminalize and dehumanize Indigenous people. These oppressive narratives impede a fair chance at justice for Indigenous victims. This is further exemplified by the fact that no Indigenous jurors were allowed to be part of the proceedings. Had there been one Indigenous juror in the proceedings, maybe the jury would have been more prone to questioning the colonial story being told during the trial.

Following the Indigenous Joint Action Coalition's (IJAC) public statement, Jade echoed their reminder to the public, "Colten Boushie is not on trial, Indigenous Peoples are not on trial. It is in fact Gerald Stanley who is on trial for the murder of Colten Boushie." Yet, to this day, we still hear people refer to it as the "Colten Boushie case." In order to disrupt the colonial story, we need to re-inform our tellings of the truth, violence and danger regarding the Colten Boushie killing and the injustice that followed. And we need to support those that stand up against the colonial story.

People like to say that there are two sides to every story, without realizing that they only tell one story and they only listen to that same story over and over again. We appreciate the work that Dallas and Gina are doing to unpack that story, to question it, to apply a critical lens to help us all understand the way colonial narratives work.

Do you believe those colonial stories? If you don't, are you silent when you hear those stories being told by people you know and love? That does its own damage and we ask you to be brave and confront, with love, the people perpetuating these harmful narratives.

The stories we tell today will inform those of tomorrow.

# PREFACE

In February of 2018, we wrote an op-ed for the *Globe and Mail* about the colonial legacies underpinning the arguments that the attorney for Gerald Stanley made in his defence of the killing of Colten Boushie—these were arguments premised on settler entitlement to property, to space, to a life free of the 'terror' occasioned by Indigenous presence. We saw that op-ed as an opportunity to educate non-Indigenous peoples on the processes of settler colonization of which their ancestors were, and, perhaps more importantly, they are currently, a part. We also intended to provide a document for Indigenous peoples, who are well aware of these processes, to perhaps view it as a resource to pass on to others. In short, our writing of the op-ed, and now this book, is not a neutral act: it emerges from the authors' own experiences growing up as Indigenous people in the prairies and reverberates outwards, to both Indigenous peoples and settlers alike.

This book is a gesture to the long histories and contemporary realities of settler colonialism in the prairies, and to how Indigenous peoples navigate and have navigated these colonial processes. Ultimately, we want to shed light on how settler colonialism narrates itself into being through processes of storytelling, and we want settlers to know these histories and how they have shaped their imaginaries, their relations, and the way they *conceive* of their relations with others (especially, in this instance, with Indigenous peoples and lands). We want this book to be an intervention, a "gift" to those reluctant to think of these issues, precisely because we do not want Indigenous youth to be subject to the violence visited upon Colten Boushie, a violence that settlers (particularly white men) seem all too ready and willing to deliver. We want to invert dominant narratives so that the theft of Colten, and other Indigenous peoples' lives, are taken as seriously as the theft of private property.

In short, we want this book to be a learning opportunity: be aware of your histories, of your stories, and then figure out what it means to take responsibility for those histories, so that you might interrupt enduring cycles of settler colonial violence. This book also offers an invitation to become attentive to the many stories of the territories you inhabit, to the geographies that house so much more than your homes, your farms, your castles. Be aware of how stories (i.e., mythologies) structure not only your daily interactions, but also the institutions that facilitate the way we interact with one another, how these mythologies might help to constitute these institutions unfairly, and how this has real, tangible, material effects for Indigenous peoples. As we explain in this book, stories can create the conditions for life on the one hand, but they can also justify the taking of life on the other.

On February 9th, 2018, a white settler farmer named Gerald Stanley was acquitted by Saskatchewan's Court of Queen's Bench for the murder of Colten Boushie, a Cree youth from the Red Pheasant First Nation in Treaty 6 territory.[1]

Colten was a passenger in a vehicle that drove onto the Stanley farm on the night of August 9th, 2016. On their way home from swimming in a river, he and a group of friends had a flat tire and drove into the Stanleys' yard in search of assistance. A series of altercations took place between the Stanley family and two of the male youths who had exited the vehicle, at which point Stanley retrieved and fired a 1947 Tokarev TT-33 handgun into the air. He would later explain that he was firing warning shots to make noise, as he did when wild animals came onto his farm and he wanted to scare them away (*R. v. Stanley* 2018, 662 & 687). By this time, Colten had moved to the driver's seat, and was trying to start the vehicle to leave the property when he was killed by Stanley, shot in the back of the head at point blank range.[2] Gerald Stanley's wife, Leesa Stanley, told the remaining youths "that's what you get for trespassing" (*R. v. Stanley* 2017, 308).

Stanley's trial saw the unfolding of a narrative that would prove powerful enough to justify his actions to an all-white jury from the Battlefords' judicial district. The narrative crafted by the defense centered around a hang-fire, 'a magical gun'[3] that misfired in "a freak accident," which occurred during what Stanley characterized as a moment of "pure terror" (*R. v. Stanley* 2018, 697). The supposed terrorists: a car full of Indigenous youth presumed to be planning to steal, or cause damage to, a quad that was parked in the Stanleys' yard.

Stanley's defense lawyer, Scott Spencer, did not explicitly argue that Stanley killed Colten in self-defense. But Stanley's version of the events—defense of his property, family, and his own life—were recurring themes throughout the trial. He described his actions as driven by a concern for the security of his adult son and wife, which gave rise to a narrative crafted around the 'chivalry' he demonstrated when confronting Indigenous youths presumed to be lawbreakers.

No one, not even Stanley himself, contested the fact that he had caused Colten's death. The defense denied that Stanley intended to shoot Colten and thus argued that he should not be convicted of second-degree murder. In addition, to avoid the lesser charge of manslaughter resulting from careless use of a gun, the defense sought to frame Stanley's conduct as "reasonable"[4] by relying upon notions of terror, panic, and the crisis that Stanley faced when he encountered a carload of Indigenous youth engaged in supposedly reckless behavior, which the defense labelled a "nightmare situation."[5] Asking the jury to "put themselves in Gerry's boots," the defense argued that Stanley's conduct was not a marked departure from the level of care that a reasonable person could be expected to exercise in similarly "nightmarish circumstances" (*R. v. Stanley* 2018, 820 & 854).

Throughout the trial Stanley's lawyers mounted a case based on notions of his industriousness and family values, repeatedly referencing the inconvenient and unfortunate disruption of wealth and prosperity Colten's death caused for the Stanley family. While extraneous to the interaction that took place between Stanley and Colten, these elements were center stage throughout the trial. Correspondingly, the defense's narrative also revolved around the "mischief" and "misadventure" that the Indigenous youth had created that day (*R. v. Stanley* 2018, 649-). These themes and elements also figured prominently in how the media reported the story and in the public discourse about the case.

The story of Colten's life also had undercurrents that were purposefully and deliberately left out of the trial and situated as extraneous factors. But they are no less important than those that were allowed by the court to characterize Stanley's version of events. Nevertheless, the nuances of Colten's story were purposefully and strategically blocked and ignored. Lost in the media soundbites and articles surrounding this trial were the ways in which this sequence of events is intimately tied to the processes of dispossession and settlement of what is currently called Canada.

We will never know the jury's rationale for acquitting Stanley on charges of both second-degree murder and manslaughter. What we do know is that the evidence offered by firearms experts did not support the hang-fire situation described by Spencer, and even if it had, Stanley was still not exercising the level of care that he should have been while using a gun. Yet the narratives constructed by the Crown were compelling enough to make his conduct appear "reasonable" in light of the supposed terror he faced.

This book, much like the dialogue surrounding the trial, isn't strictly focused on the death of Colten or the trial of Stanley. What we are interested in are the affective and material realities of the narratives surrounding Colten's death. This is particularly important because the prairies, and white rural Saskatchewan in particular, are marked by mythical tropes about the virtuousness of its people and the righteousness of its political and cultural formations. Indigenous people are outside of these myths, except when we can be invoked in ways that bolster them. Instead, there are many tropes about Indigenous people that function to naturalize our exclusion, immiseration, and ultimately, death.

Throughout this book, we use the term 'storying' to describe the ways in which narratives, or spoken and written accounts, come alive and function as important political tools. We are indebted to feminists and Indigenous people for drawing attention to the power of storytelling relative to lived experience. Julie Cruikshank writes that "the question of which versions of a story are "correct" may be less interesting than what each story reveals about the cultural values of its narrator[s]" (2003, 433). As the Stanley case demonstrates, the "values" held by settlers on the prairies can work to legitimatize violence against Indigenous people at societal and institutional levels. This book shows the very real danger of the dialogue in and surrounding Stanley's trial by exploring the schismatic relationship between Indigenous and non-Indigenous peoples, in the prairies in particular, and in Canada more broadly.

Nowhere has this relational crisis been more clearly exemplified, at a societal level, than in the comments sections of media articles, in online forums, or on Twitter. After Colten's death, in the lead up to the trial, during the trial, and in the long shadow of its aftermath, a virulent onslaught of hate and racism flourished and continues to flourish online. It is rarely—if ever—checked or mediated by anyone. The public discourse engendered and sustained by the trial viewed the case as an issue of crime and property that both drew on and reproduced colonial representations of Indigenous deviance and inferiority. This bolstered settler calls for a solution to 'the Indian problem' not found in the legal system, justifying the use of extra-legal violence or vigilantism among some settler groups, and simultaneously reproducing racialized notions of criminality, terror, and culpability.

Indeed, the news release issued by the RCMP after Colten's death framed the interactions and events on the Stanley farm as a death associated with a theft-related incident.[6]

The initial police response to, and investigation of, the killing of Colten Boushie on the Stanley farm made clear that Colten's death did not merit the same consideration and sympathy afforded to white victims and their families, due to his presumed complicity in his friends' actions, and thus, his culpability in creating the circumstances that led to his own death. In many ways, Colten's death and the Stanley trial are symptomatic of a larger settler colonial system; they illustrate enduring asymmetrical structural patterns of relationships between Indigenous and settler peoples on the prairies. In them, we see how the dispossession of territories and lives continues to manifest in the present, as well as how this dispossession is naturalized and normalized. Indeed, it is difficult to understand the outcome of the trial outside of these colonial conditions. This is why to many anonymous racist internet commentators, and one person later identified as an RCMP officer, Colten "got what he deserved" (Martens and Roache 2018). It was, to them, the 'natural' order of things, which is to say, the past colliding with the present, or what Christina Sharpe calls "the past that is not past" (2016).

*Storying Violence* explores the structure and operations of colonialism in the prairies, a process that is historic, ongoing, and systemic; it organizes nearly every realm of social, political, and economic life at multiple scales. It intersects with sexism and cis-heteronormativity, forming a white settler masculine ethos that shapes Indigenous-settler relations and the ideas settlers held and still hold about Indigenous communities. Despite the pervasiveness of these colonial operations, they remain invisible to many people, enabled by racialized, capitalist, and heteropatriarchal logics and norms.

Our aim is to unsettle dominant accounts of Colten's death, framed by narratives of settler life in the prairies, and centre instead the experiences of Indigenous peoples. We focus on the particular ways that racialized and colonial logics have shaped Indigenous and non-Indigenous relations in these spaces. To do this, we historicize the present by exploring the operations of discourses of white superiority and Indigenous inferiority in Saskatchewan over time and by explaining how these continue to shape contemporary relations in these geographies. We deliberately place a spotlight on that which forms the supposedly invisible backdrop of oppression, interrogating the taken for granted assumptions about Indigenous peoples that exist in the prairies and explaining the ways in which they function to configure the lives of all those who reside here.

Concurrently, we recognize that the voices and stories of Indigenous peoples are, more often than not, downplayed, obscured by, or not taken into account at all within dominant narratives. Indigenous peoples' experiences are too often narrated by those who have not experienced colonialism firsthand. Thus, we deliberately construct an account of prairie relationships that centers Indigenous peoples' experiences, drawing on the accounts of the Boushie family but also broadly on our own upbringings as Indigenous people in Treaty 4 and 8.[7]

This book will proceed by identifying and unravelling the narratives, or stories, that structure the events that took place on the Stanley farm on August 9th, 2016. Chapter 1, "Storying the Prairie West," attends to the longstanding myths Canada tells about itself and the settlement of the prairies. In Chapter 2, we outline the effacement of "race" in the trial of Stanley (the way it becomes framed as "The Case That's 'Not About Race'"), and how this worked strategically to limit or prohibit discussions of racism in a geography that is deeply structured by racial violence. The third Chapter, "Whites 'Coveted Indian Land but not Land with Indians on It'," details the endless drive of settler colonialism to rid Indigenous territories of Indigenous peoples, and to eliminate Indigenous communities in order to replace them with a settler colonial order with its own forms of law and governance. Finally, in Chapter 4, we articulate how "settler reason" becomes the normative project and logic of the prairies, and how this allows for the violences of settler colonialism to continue. In Chapter 4 and the Conclusion we suggest that the logics of treaty, and the potential relations embedded therein, provide important inspiration for the imagination of alternate configurations of relationship in the prairies. We consider how this renewed emphasis on treaty might change how Indigenous peoples and non-Indigenous peoples interact with one another, and how this might in turn mitigate or prevent future violence. This project, ultimately, stories the contours of violence in order to resist it.

Specifically, this book takes up the relations between Indigenous and non-Indigenous peoples in the prairies in order to critically engage the narratives that figure prominently surrounding the death of Colten Boushie. It also carves out space for the stories of Indigenous resistance and refusal that have always been present but are situated outside of or in opposition to settler tropes.

# 1

# *Storying the Prairie West*

*Those that come after us in the Government will think of your children as we think of you.*

—Treaty Commissioner Alexander Morris (1880, 210)

*Every Canadian will gain if we escape the impasse that breeds confrontation between Aboriginal and non-Aboriginal people across barricades, real or symbolic. But the barricades will not fall until we understand how they were built.*

—Royal Commission on Aboriginal People

As the quintessential Canadian settlement story goes, early European newcomers arrived in North America and entered into respectful and mutually-beneficial trade and diplomatic relations with Indigenous populations. This story of peaceful settlement and development either highlights Indigenous consent to the theft of our land and cession of our political authority, or glosses over it under the guise of partnership and nation-building. Indigenous people, and Indigenous women in particular, are represented as brokers of cultural difference, those who both metaphorically and literally birthed "the hybridity" which Canada has since claimed as its origin story.[8]

Such characterizations are a recurring theme in the seemingly endless search for the holy grail of a peaceful, prosperous Canadian identity. To be clear, this national identity is an imaginary construct, yet the fact that consecutive generations of hopeful Canadians have exacted, rationalized, and concealed violence in its name deems it worthy of further inquiry. Here we include the myriad violences against Indigenous peoples that have been committed and that continue to be committed in the interest of assimilation/integration, under the guise of liberal multicultural imperatives of equality and tolerance, and/or other political ideals pursued in the service of the Canadian 'national interest.'

Following early trade relations with Indigenous peoples in the prairies, the Crown is said to have negotiated consensual land-cession treaties with Indigenous populations. This purportedly opened the prairie west up for settlement in exchange for the promise of civilization and, protection. In the popular record, this is where Indigenous peoples' contribution to the creation of Canada effectively ends, at least at a symbolic level. We were either perceived to be rapidly dying off, effectively conquered, relocated to and content with life on reserves, or absorbed into the Canadian body politic. Here we see multiple narratives operating in tandem: the myth of the vanishing Indian, the narrative of the irrelevant/incidental Indian as part of the myth of elimination (some Indians might remain, but settlers need not worry about them or their counter-claims), and if they become a problem, then the 'murderable Indian', whereby violence is justified in the name of progress and prosperity. However—as with any story—this isn't the only version.

More telling than the stories that are represented in dominant narratives are the accounts that aren't heard. These are stories of land theft, genocide, gendered violence, and dispossession. For the settler story to exist as 'reality', other experiences that contradict it must be bracketed or dismissed as 'alternate versions', as narratives that solely appeal to sympathetic 'bleeding heart' progressives, as biased because they reflect Indigenous experiences, as hypocritical if they deviate from caricatures of pre-contact Indigenous life, as historical grievances that we should 'just move on from', or as the result of co-optation by external parties interested in utilizing Indigenous suffering to leverage their own political agendas.

This ensures Indigenous experiences are either drastically downplayed or dismissed as identity politics, as the ramblings of a minority or 'special interest group' that poses a threat to the national interest.

This zero-sum dynamic also manifests in face-offs between competing conceptions of governance, law, social relations, economy, and the relationship between humans and the lands and waterways. In all of these realms, Indigenous ways of seeing the world and our ways of being are represented as a threat to settler ways of life. The drive to eliminate Indigenous people *as Indigenous* is quite literally part of the foundational structure of the Canadian nation. Of course, this eliminatory logic targets Indigenous bodies not just because of our physical presence, but because of our alterity.[9]

Even as Indigenous populations have grown in numbers and in social and political presence, settlers seeking to achieve 'the good life' in the prairies have continued to trample over our rights as Indigenous peoples and as human beings. This can be seen in efforts to deny the existence of our distinct rights, to mischaracterize them, terminate them, restrict our ability to exercise them, or to find ways to "justifiably" infringe upon them. In so doing, they have drawn on capitalist, racist, and misogynist ideologies and imperatives to rationalize the denial of our freedom and aspirations.

At other times, Indigenous peoples have been encouraged to join the 'prairie good life' by way of invitation or forcible incorporation into settler society, and to become the type of citizens to whom Canada promises prosperity, security, and an adequate standard of living.

The latter approach has taken many forms—enfranchisement, assimilation, 'self-government' arrangements, invitations to 'join the modern economy,' and so on. Despite growing calls for the inclusion of Indigenous people and our perspectives within dominant institutions, these forms of recognition only serve to graft Indigenous peoples onto the story of a prosperous Canadian existence, to buy into a conception of the 'good life' within overarching terms and power-relations that are not of our own choosing, and that require us to relinquish the relations with Creation that inform who we are as Indigenous peoples.

## 'Settling' the Plains:
## A Story of Newcomer Health and Wealth

From the late 1800s to the early 1900s, Canadian government officials initiated an immigration campaign dedicated to attracting European and American settlers to the prairie provinces of Manitoba, Saskatchewan and Alberta.

Early immigration materials described the prairie west as a vast, unoccupied, fertile hinterland with little, if any, mention of Indigenous populations. Colonial settlements offered newcomers property, bounty, independence, industry, and most of all, opportunities for wealth that would vastly exceed those available in their countries of origin.

The cover images of magazines such as "Canada West" generally depicted idealized notions of western life, and while the imagery

"Canada the New Homeland" Poster reproduced in Canada West. 1925.
Source: Library and Archives Canada, item no.: 2958967.

evolved over the years that they were in circulation, there were several specific messages that were consistently delivered. We linger on these symbols because they provide an important window into the particular operations and configurations of prairie settler colonialism—in a way, they typify the story of the settlement of the west, both in what they depict and what they exclude.

First, the west was depicted as an unparalleled "land of opportunity" that potential settlers were invited to join. The notion of opportunity is entangled with capitalist logics, promising newcomers the ability to accumulate wealth and property to their hearts' content, with little, if anything, standing in their way. Magazine covers showed an open and uninhabited prairie setting—a blue sky, lush greenery, thriving wheat fields and farm animals, all in an expansive and empty geography free of any Indigenous peoples.

---

"Canadian National Railways. A Home and Success in Canada." (ca. 1920-1935). The text reads: "Why not seek a new home on the land in Canada? In the World's Granary the best of land is cheap and a man may reasonably hope to work his way to independence. The Canadian National Railways' Colonization Department helps new settlers, meeting them on arrival, and securing farm employment for them." Source: Glenbow Museum, file no.: Poster-19.

"Ready Made Farms in Western Canada" Canadian Pacific Railway Advertisement, (ca. 1910-1930). Source: Glenbow Archives, reference code: glen-3257-is-glen-1342.

The environment is often described as "rich virgin soil," as "fertile plains," and a "climate [that is] the healthiest in the world." In many ways this appealed to prevailing masculinist impulses geared towards exploration, occupation, and cultivation. Some posters advertised very affordable or even free land, while others offered cash incentives to settle in western provinces (known at the time as Manitoba and the Northwest Territories). The images often included written descriptions of the prairies as "the new Eldorado" and "the last best west," likely in reference to the US plains that had already experienced massive annexation, expropriation, and subsequent occupation by newcomers, and thus had less land "available for settlement." Some ads also promised specific opportunities, such as the proximity to coal fields or to the railway, implying easy accessibility to urban centers and distant markets.

Cover of Canada West, 1923. Source: Glenbow Museum, file no.: 971-2-C212c-1923.

Cover of Canada West: "Canada - The New Homeland," 1930. Source: Glenbow Museum, File no.: 971-2-C212c-1930.

"Red Star Line. Southampton-Canada via Cherbourg," (ca. 1910-1930). Source: Glenbow Museum, file no.: Poster-23.

Notably, this messaging targeted immigration to the rural prairies rather than urban centers. Prairie farmers were needed to produce grains for domestic use and international export, and to provide a market for the manufacturers of eastern and central Canada (Conway 2014, 38-39). While the east was intended to be a hub of industry, the architects of settler policy envisioned the west as a region that would produce much needed resources to support the country's economy (ideas that still resonate today, especially with Alberta and Saskatchewan residents' repeated threats to "separate" from the rest of Canada). Prairie populations would produce goods, while also ensuring traffic for the railways (Palmer 1992, 310). As John Belshaw notes, "The CPR [Canadian Pacific Railroad] owned much of the arable right-of-way between Lake Superior and the Rockies, so settlers enriched the Railway as customers and as tenants or purchasers of land" (2016).

The intended role of the prairie settler is apparent in a 1921 issue of *Canada West* magazine, which described city life:

[The worker] is but a cog in the great commercial wheel and one who has failed to give his true condition proper and just consideration. With an equal loyalty to his daily pursuits, and but a part of the energy displayed in the city, he could reap all the

"The Last Best West" Cover of Pamphlet Canada West, produced by the Dept. of The Interior 1909. Source: Library and Archives Canada, item no.: 2958968.

advantages of life with its personal and financial independence by becoming a producer—a farm owner (Chandler 2016).

The self-reliant farm owner was in the service of no one but himself and the land he cultivated. He could raise a family in peaceful green fields, with little of the encumbrances of urban life. He was, to use a well-worn cliché, king of his castle on the plains.

Secondly, these images are noteworthy for the highly gendered and heteronormative ideals that they embody; namely, normative ideas of the family, home, and domestic life. The imagery idealizes a heterosexual, patriarchal, agrarian, nuclear family unit. An able-bodied, middle-aged white farmer is typically the central figure in these images, often with his beautiful young wife and a son in his hands. In the background is an image of the wide-open prairies upon which his property—"his castle"—

lies. These images simultaneously appeal to and uphold the institution of masculinity: the ability to build a home, provide for and protect one's family, and most importantly, to exercise control over one's private domain. This private domain purportedly exists and is bound within a lawless land, with the farmer serving as king of this realm, and whose responsibility it then becomes to protect

"It's Mine: The Right Land for the Right Man. Canadian National Railways advertisement (circa 1920-1935). Source: Glenbow Archives, ref. code: glen-3257-is-glen-1338.

GINA STARBLANKET & DALLAS HUNT

against intrusions into this estate or disruptions of this narrative. Targeted to those who could hold and pass on property, the posters also emphasized the male head of household's possessory rights, featuring phrases such as "the right land for the right man," or by depicting the image of a farmer declaring "my land!" or "it's mine."

Third, these images illustrate the ways in which settler colonial states incentivize newcomers to take up the land that Indigenous peoples have ancestral and ongoing relationships with. This is a practice of dispossession and political subordination. After all, what better way to guard against Indigenous claims to our ancestral territories than to give that very land away to newcomers and facilitate its conversion to private property? Here we recall Duncan Campbell Scott's visualization of purportedly 'ceded land' across Canada as "like a patchwork blanket; as far north as the confines of the new provinces of Saskatchewan and Alberta the patches lie edge to edge" (1906).

Agrarian settlement cemented Indigenous dispossession across the prairies, rather than simply within urban centres, as newcomers would take up expansive tracts of land there and their survival would directly depend upon their ability to independently own, develop, and secure the land. Once it "belonged" to settler farmers, Indigenous peoples could be framed as criminals or, to invoke the depictions used in the Stanley case, as intruders, merely for our continued presence on the lands that we belong to.

Indeed, some of the posters emphasize the safety that would be provided to settlers through the implementation of Western forms of law and order. They declare there is "nothing to fear, protected by the government."

Blanketing the plains with settler homesteads would quickly extend Canada's political reach, as Canada's 'proper' settler citizens would then lay claim to huge tracts of land relative to the amount of territory taken up by settlers in urban spaces. This, in turn, would serve to delimit Indigenous peoples' claims to the land, as private property would eventually be 'off-the-table' for Indigenous 'land claims.' As Belshaw writes, both settlement and the railways in Canada can be understood as a "strategy for asserting sovereignty across the West against American and Aboriginal ambitions and counter claims" (2016).

The presence of settler populations that would eventually outnumber Indigenous peoples, and that held both property interests and political influence that Indigenous peoples were denied, bolstered the need for Indigenous repression, dispossession, disciplining, and assimilation. But they would also give way to the proliferation of normative assumptions and ideas about the roles of settler citizens and the roles of Indigenous people in the prairies.

These images demonstrate the inner-workings of the logic of elimination; that is, they proliferate the notion that Indigenous

"Western Canada: The New Eldorado," (ca. 1890-1920). Source: Library and Archives Canada, MIKAN 2945432.

peoples have either disappeared from the prairies, or that Indigenous people who do exist in these spaces are not relevant or significant considerations for a newcomer society.

Colonial settlement narratives either expunged Indigenous peoples entirely from portrayals of prairie life, or when they did appear, they were described as occupying a role that would not interfere with the agrarian settler lifestyle.

In one of the few immigration handbooks that had any mention of Indigenous peoples living in these territories, they were described as "quiet" and "inoffensive" with "hunting grounds in the far back of the North-West" (1874, 44). Here Indigenous peoples are positioned as being distracted by cultural practices that only require peripheral relationships with the landscape and that promise not to interfere with the ability of settlers to enjoy their new homeland. Prairie newcomers were essentially directed not to take seriously Indigenous peoples' rights or our ongoing relationships with the geographies that were being offered to potential settlers.

And, these images illustrate the type of citizen that Canada sought to attract to the prairie west, leaving no doubt that settlement in these spaces was, from the outset, driven by racialized, classist, and gendered logics geared towards cultivating a 'progressive,' idealized civilization.[10] As Howard Palmer states, the Canadian elite "had been taught to believe that the Anglo-Saxon peoples and British principles of government were the apex of both biological evolution and human achievement, and they believed that Canada's greatness was due in large part to its

Anglo-Saxon heritage" (1992, 311). Prairie immigration policies, in particular, were driven by perceived racial, cultural, and religious hierarchies that situated some prospective settlers as more desirable than others. These decisions surrounding racialized inclusion/exclusion were justified through the notion that some populations would fare better in the cold, harsh climate, or be better equipped to take on the hard labour of rural life than other populations (Asaka 2017).

From the decline of the fur trade onwards, Canada's national policy was increasingly shaped by and in favour of the desire to create a nation of permanent settler populations, which required Canadian officials to shore up territory, legibility, and legitimacy, not only for Canada's subjects, but also for other (especially neighbouring) nations. As Wotherspoon and Satzewich explain, the Crown's approach to relations with Indigenous peoples was grounded on its own fluctuating needs as determined by shifting processes of accumulation of capital (2000, 18-28). Canada's early approach to Indian affairs was not necessarily concerned with the need for permanent settlements, and in fact sought to interfere less with Indigenous peoples' relationship with the land as these were crucial to the fur trade. However, the shift from mercantile to industrial capitalism required the separation of Indigenous peoples from the land and its conversion to private property in order to make it available for settlement and new forms of exploitation.

Moreover, these idealized visions of permanent settler societies were driven by racialized logics. Where early settlers came

GINA STARBLANKET & DALLAS HUNT

primarily from Europe, from 1897 – 1913 Clifford Sifton's immigration policies also sought to attract settlers from the United States, notably American, Scandinavian, and German people who were already living there. These populations had already acquired the necessary agricultural skills to thrive in the west; they were perceived to have close racial and cultural characteristics, and were viewed as hard working, industrious people of high character; this was precisely the sort of citizen Canadian government officials desired for the prairies (Friesen 1987, 244; Palmer 1992, 313).

In short, prairie immigration campaigns were targeted at individuals and populations that would most easily lead to the creation of civilized, agrarian societies envisioned by officials. British standards informed the conception of what "a good life" would be in the west, and also shaped officials' impressions of the suitability of prospective settlers, in terms of their physical appearance and cultural values. At the same time, immigration from populations who were seen to be of greater cultural and racial distance, or lacking the proper climatic temperament, such as Chinese, Japanese, Italian, Jewish, and Black populations, was largely discouraged (Friesen 1987, 246).

Basically, the images produced, perpetuated, and appealed to ideas and ideals that prioritized a form of settlement that heavily romanticized prairie life in an effort to expand the Canadian state's reach as well as its legitimacy across the landscape. The ideologies appealed to and cultivated were (and continue to be today) decidedly racialized and ethnocentric, masculinist, heteronormative, driven by capitalist ideologies, and built upon the notion that Indigenous peoples have vacated these spaces and thus it is just the wild and underutilized geography that needs to be conquered. The current state of Indigenous and non-Indigenous relations in the prairies and in other spaces find their origins in these integrated and ongoing patterns and stories of colonial settlement and Indigenous displacement; neither can be divorced from the other.

It is important to recognize that these images are not just representative of the intentions of the architects of Canada's national policy, but that they also illustrate the norms, values, expectations, and aspirations that were held by individual settlers and subsequently inherited by their descendants. They form an often invisible, taken for granted backdrop of prairie life, yet one that bears further consideration as it speaks to the ideals, beliefs, and desires that contemporary settlers hold, and that in turn informs a negative perception of those who disrupt this narrative. Indeed, these images can be said to be cultivating or constituting something resembling a prairie settler "common sense."[11]

## *Establishing Civil Societies in a State of Nature*

Taken together, the racialized and gendered nature of early colonial rhetoric would be a crucial part of the establishment of permanent settler colonies. The creation of a new settler society could not, contrary to popular narratives of peaceful settlement and development, be built through the establishment of relationships of equality between Indigenous and non-Indigenous peoples. As explained above, along with the declining profitability of the fur trade, colonial policies were increasingly geared towards the need to build permanent rather than temporary settlements of Europeans. This, in turn, necessitated the institution of more marked racial and gendered hierarchies between Indigenous and non-Indigenous people. Adele Perry contextualizes this shift in social interactions; where intimate and marital relations between Indigenous and non-Indigenous people were fruitful during the fur trade, the project of nation-building would require a "proper separation of races" (1997: 506). Indeed, by the mid to late 1800s, white men were being instructed not to marry Indigenous women, and were encouraged instead to "assert [their] own superiority by ceasing to associate with [Indigenous peoples] on equal terms, and let them feel themselves to be what they really are—less than civilized and far worse than savage" (Perry 1997, 206, quoting I.D.C. 1862).

Throughout the 18th and 19th centuries, scientific theories of race provided the justification for the right of Europeans to rule over 'uncivilized' people and also served as the foundation for colonial hierarchies (Backhouse 1999, 5). That is, racial classifications provided the explanation and rationalization for the subordination of groups of people deemed to be inferior. These classifications are not merely ideological but also deeply material in that they were and still are invoked to explain "why certain groups of people were entitled to hold inequitable resources, status, and power over others" (Backhouse 1999, 6). In the absence of social hierarchies, it would be difficult to explain how and why settler newcomers had the authority to assert sovereignty and jurisdiction over Indigenous people who lived in the prairie region for countless generations. In short, these social hierarchies had to be entrenched and reproduced; they had to be naturalized and normalized as the ongoing narrative of the prairie west. This is part of the process of "storying."

Colonialism, both past and present, has relied upon notions of progress, development, and civilization to provide the ideological justification for the extension of settler laws and regulations of Indigenous peoples and their lands. Standards of civilization are based on a temporal distinction that casts Indigenous peoples as inhabiting a primitive state that is earlier on an evolutionary scale, in comparison to the more advanced or 'modern' existence of western states. This distinction renders Euro-western governance as the only legitimate political formation and locks Indigenous prerogatives in the past by seeing us as uncivilized, primitive, and less developed than European people (Arneil 1996; Tully 1995). It also positions Indigenous peoples as dependent on the goodwill of settlers to bring us into a more advanced period to ensure our survival.

James Youngblood Henderson has written how by the eighteenth century, the usual explanation of the origin of the state, or "civil society," began by advancing an original state of nature in which primitive humans lived on their own and were subject to neither government nor law (2000, 28). The prairie west was in many ways understood as originally being in a "state of nature" with inhabitants that needed to be civilized, instituting a distinction between savagery and civility in ways that has continued to shape the imaginaries of those who reside in the prairies over time. Notably, these assumptions coalesced with religious ideals in the aim of eliminating Indigenous "deficiencies" through the residential school system, though they are not exclusive to a form of xenophobic Christianity. The protection of property was seen to be a hallmark of civil society, and the imperative to secure and improve one's property became one of the primary motivations for and functions of government.

In this story of the "state of nature," individuals had to work to preserve their own life and their own livelihood, which thus made it a dangerous setting as there were no limits on the degree to which self-preservation could be carried out. In civil society, by contrast, individuals agreed to enter into a social contract whereby they gave up certain rights in exchange for the protection of their property rights. A life of 'civility' was seen to be universally desirable, and early colonial officials presumed that Indigenous people would voluntarily trade our lives (in a "state of nature") in exchange for the promises and protections of civil society. However, the only individuals who would find such protections would be those who relinquished their Indigenous culture and identity and became members of Canadian society.

European settlers were arriving to the prairies with the assumption that they would be able to live a 'civil life', and a hierarchical order would allow them to pursue a good and prosperous settler existence, unencumbered by concern for those who were killed or displaced in the name of this 'nation-building' process. In particular, the cultivation and proliferation of settler understandings of white supremacy and Indigenous deficiency would help justify and rationalize the violence inherent in this process as necessary for the protection of the new nation's proper citizenry.

Today, we continue to see the operations of these logics, whereby Indigenous lives are seen to be of lesser value for our perceived failure to integrate with or properly contribute to neighboring non-Indigenous communities. While the civilized/uncivilized distinction has been widely discredited at a theoretical level, it remains alive and well in practice and in story (LaRocque 2010). It gets deployed through coded language that depicts Indigenous people as 'lawless' or as 'threats' to those deserving of the protections afforded by civil society.

In addition, many of the public opinions surrounding the youths' presence on the Stanley farm on the day of Colten's death, such as the suggestion that Indigenous people should 'get an education,' 'find productive ways to pass their days,' 'pay taxes' and 'contribute more to society,' all speak to the continuation of these colonial logics—they speak to the type of storying that consistently and constantly absents Indigenous peoples from the prairie west, or else. That is to say, if we are not absent, if we stake a claim to our ongoing presence, then we disrupt the narratives of the man and his castle, and in so doing, face the violence we purportedly "deserve."

# 2

# The Case That's "Not About Race"

[W]hite colonial paranoia, injury, and worrying are inextricably tied to an anxiety about dispossession.

—Aileen Moreton-Robinson (2015, 152)

Canada—past and present—is a settler colonial political formation. This truth is increasingly recognized by well-informed individuals. Unfortunately, not all who make their home in Canada are informed.

And, even among those who are informed, even fewer people recognize the ways in which they are implicated by, and in many cases, benefit from, contemporary structures of colonialism in everyday and innumerable ways.

Many people—informed and uninformed—see their every-day actions as divorced from colonial governing systems and institutions; many see themselves as independently self-made individuals unburdened by the violence of the colonial histories that have produced the present. But colonialism forms a scaffolding that is largely invisible to those who do not experience its harmful consequences firsthand or who deny its connection to the disproportionate levels of suffering faced by Indigenous peoples.

Thus non-Indigenous people can claim to see colonialism without ever feeling compelled to transform it. They can perceive the story, the narrative of colonization, without ever having to, or even feeling the need to, work to change its regenerative structures or foundations.

## *The Particulars of Settler Colonial Logics in the Prairies*

Over the past few decades, much effort has been dedicated to exploring the inner-workings of various colonial contexts, as scholars have attempted to map out the commonalities but also differences in the ways that colonialism structures Indigenous and non-Indigenous relations across locations, each with their own distinct social, political, and economic characteristics.[12]

Within Canada too, settler colonialism takes shape in distinct contexts and historical moments. Some foundational aspects are shared, such as the fact that colonialism is structurally embedded and ongoing, that it operates through an eliminatory logic, that it is heavily racialized and sexualized, and that its driving motivation is land.[13] And while the removal and containment of Indigenous peoples was and continues to be motivated by the settler drive to claim the lands, waters, and the rest of creation as their own, the particular way in which land dispossession is carried out is not identical within settler states; that is, settler states use a variety of tactics and strategies to achieve these goals. These inform the creation of regional political cultures that can contextualize the differences between settler political ideas and values across Canada, and that also shed light on the differences that exist in settler-Indigenous political relations across regions.

At least some of the distinctions in how colonialism plays out can be identified by looking at the particular relationships between colonial states and the types of commodities they seek to access and exploit. In contexts of settler colonialism, this commodity is, as we have already mentioned, the land, but also access to the land as a precondition to access and exploit other materials, including 'natural resources' and labour, among other things.

Yet the particular relationships that different settler populations have with the living earth vary across geographies. Paraphrasing Sarah Rotz (2017), specific histories, proximities, and relations to land and resources represent important factors that condition systemic hierarchies and are brought to life in the spaces between actors. The way in which settler livelihoods are situated relative to the ability to access and derive a profit from land instantiates not just a particular relationship with the land but also with Indigenous peoples whose prior assertions to those same territories may conflict with or threaten settler access. In other words, the material differences in how settler colonialism plays out in different regions of Canada can be revealed by looking, at least in part, to the various ideals that settlers initially held and continue to hold relative to particular geographies and how these collide or come into tension with Indigenous understandings of our relationship with and responsibilities toward the earth.

What we're suggesting is that questions of land theft must be understood contextually and that, contrary to nearly every government proposal surrounding Indigenous-settler relations in Canada, there is no universal or national way of conceptualizing these relations given that the foundational crises themselves manifest in different ways. Rather, we must engage context-specific analyses of the relationships between Indigenous and non-Indigenous peoples through an understanding that is informed by each of these populations' local political cultures, and the particular needs and aspirations of both Indigenous and non-Indigenous populations in regions across the country. One way of contextualizing colonial relations is by examining how the logics and processes of racialization operate differently across different geographies.

In settler colonial states, racialization functions as a means of "imposing classificatory grids on a variety of colonized populations" (Wolfe 2016, 10). However, racialization is also not a monolithic, decontextualized process. Even within a single country, racialization does not operate in the same way across different contexts. Thus, we need to unpack the ways that *generalized* patterns and practices of racism are *locally* enacted (Day, 2016; Wilderson, 2010). How is the racialization of Indigenous peoples constructed and managed in different regions? Why do particular forms of racialization appear in some places, and not others? How do these different forms of racialization in turn give rise to different strategies of resistance by Indigenous peoples?

Finally, one of the core aspects of settler colonialism is that it operates through an eliminatory logic. Elimination can take a variety of forms but it generally involves both "negative" or "reductive" and "positive" or "productive" elements; as Heidi Stark writes, "settler colonialism, then is not just reductive, it is productive, actively producing both the settler state and its accompanying legitimating narratives" (2016, 8). Of course, the active production of settler colonial societies means that this process is ongoing and is constantly being configured by the settler desire to access and exploit the land in the face of new and shifting political contexts.

But the way in which this eliminatory logic manifests is not uniform and can take a variety of shapes, from physical death and violence to assimilatory efforts and policies of hyperdescent, to the repression of Indigenous rights to land, and so on. Thus, in thinking about the particulars of settler colonialism in the prairies, we might think about the different ways in which elimination is envisioned, the various forms through which it materializes, the different strategies used to realize it, and the stereotypes and assumptions that eliminatory logics function to uphold.

This approach is not intended to suggest that settler colonialism, or racism, is better or worse in different areas of Canada. Rather, that there are important differences in how these systems of oppression manifest, and that identifying these distinctions may help us all understand more clearly, and thus be better positioned to respond to, the popular racism, ethnocentrism, and sexism that contribute to the multi-dimensional crises of relationship that mark Indigenous and settler peoples' lives.

## Treaty Mythologies

So far, this book has described land theft and the drive to eliminate Indigenous people as interrelated elements of the structure of settler colonialism. As the institutional practice of dispossession has taken different forms in particular regions, we have also emphasized the need to recognize the specific ways in which dispossession is carried out and maintained within specific territories. Importantly, one of the primary mechanisms that the Canadian government and people have employed to conceal or 'soften' land theft in the prairies has been through the proliferation of one-sided, Eurocentric interpretations of the numbered treaties. The Red Pheasant First Nation and the Stanley farm are both located in Treaty 6 territory, and so any discussion of the relationship between Indigenous and non-Indigenous people in these spaces must be grounded in Treaty 6 as a living, breathing agreement that governs the relationship.

The numbered treaties were negotiated from 1871-1921, as Indigenous people in the prairies were faced with an influx of settlers and rapidly declining population of buffalo and other wild animals that were crucial to our traditional lifeways. Where the numbered treaties have been signed, Indigenous peoples agreed to share the land with newcomers but only up to the depth of a plow and in exchange for commitments from the Crown. While many Indigenous leaders were hesitant to enter into treaty relationships during the negotiation of Treaty 6, they were also mindful of the impacts that their choices would have on generations to come and sought to craft relationships with newcomers that would allow Indigenous and non-Indigenous people to live alongside and learn from one another without either being subordinate to the other (Taylor, 1985, Cardinal and Hildrebrandt, 2000).

For the most part, treaties have not been implemented in accordance with the way in which they were understood by Indigenous people, but have been confined to one-sided, Eurocentric mythologies surrounding their nature and intent. Popular assumptions surrounding the numbered treaties operate to bolster settler perceptions that both the land and Indigenous political authority have been surrendered long ago, and that treaties were one-time transactions with little bearing upon contemporary settlers who reside in the prairies. Of course, the presumption that land could be converted into private property and exchanged for a fixed set of terms is one that flows from Canadian laws and worldviews, and is inconsistent with

Indigenous laws and worldviews. It is important to understand this imposition of Canadian law on top of Indigenous law as a technique of elimination, but also as the grounds for the ongoing political mobilization of Indigenous peoples in the prairies who have always resisted a transactional understanding of treaties.

It is now well-recognized by historians, anthropologists and political scientists, among others that the written version of treaties only captures part of the conversations that took place during treaty negotiations, and also distorts much of what was actually discussed.[14] Further, the written records of treaty negotiations (not the text of written treaties) have been proven to align much more closely with Indigenous understandings of what was agreed upon during treaty negotiations (Asch 2014).

Settler treaty mythologies, then, can be understood as the selective construction and misrepresentation of treaties that originate from, but are also continually reproduced through, Canadian institutions and society (Starblanket, 2019; Green, 1995). Such mythologies are wide-ranging and configure dominant representations in multiple ways. Some situate treaties as one-time events through which Indigenous peoples consensually agreed to relinquish our rights to the land and to legal and political jurisdiction in exchange for a fixed set of terms. Interpreted in this way, treaties represent mechanisms of extinguishment of Indigenous claims against Canada's assertion of sovereignty across much of the prairie west.

Another myth is that of Indigenous peoples' willing assimilation through treaty-making, that Indigenous people agreed to relinquish our ancestral relationships with creation and our traditional ways of being in exchange for the promises of civilization that Europeans would bring. And yet another myth is the economic development approach to treaty—that we were effectively 'selling' our rights to the land in the name of immediate monetary gain and economic opportunities. And finally, there is a tendency to shroud treaties in the myth of non-resistance; that is, the notion that Indigenous people passively accepted to submit to the Crown rather than engage in complex forms of political decision making and action to prevent further incursion into our lives.

Each of these mythologies have substantial material implications in the present. For instance, the persistent, Eurocentric mis-framing of treaties as land transactions instead of relationship frameworks deflects from unaddressed issues in the treaty relationship, such as outstanding land claims, jurisdictional issues, Indigenous legal and political subordination, and deeply sedimented inter-societal tensions between Indigenous and non-Indigenous people in the prairies.

To be clear, not all settlers are unaware of these outstanding issues; some advocate for the implementation of treaties in the contemporary context on the basis that it will be in the national interest to to reconcile the relationship and bring Indigenous people into the modern economy. Yet, treaty implementation is rarely contemplated in settler society in a way that allows for a return of our jurisdiction or land, or even to place limits on provincial or federal government authority.[15] By understanding the role of treaties in the prairies, we are able to contemplate how they are invoked strategically in the contemporary context as a means of protecting the national interest, and deployed in an effort to advance Indigenous incorporation into the Canadian state.

The discourse surrounding treaties can shed light on the specific workings of settler colonialism in the prairies, and in particular, on contemporary socio-political divides, as they explain the differences in the ways that settlers and Indigenous peoples understand their respective relationships to these lands. As well, it illuminates the ways in which those different understandings collide to sustain particular and often negative understandings of one another (settlers, as thieves of land, and Indigenous peoples, as having their rights extinguished through treaty and thus as entitled to demands for assistance, 'handouts,' etc). To the extent that they reinforce a mythology of consensual settler land acquisition and settlement which delegitimizes Indigenous claims against the state, narrow representations of treaties work to enable land theft and the violence against Indigenous people in the prairies. In other contexts, the process of land theft looks quite different, as do societal perceptions of the legitimacy of Indigenous peoples' political positions and assertions.

## *A Quasi-Military Police Force*
Following treaty-making, Canada sought to bolster its own legitimacy and authority by gradually placing bounds on Indigenous sovereignty and political authority through the criminalization

and domestication of Indigenous people (Stark 2016). Indeed, after the Northwest Rebellion in the area of Fort Battleford in 1885, and the subsequent hangings of those who took part, Prime Minister John A. Macdonald remarked in a letter to Edgar Dewdney that "the executions...ought to convince the Red Man that the White Man governs" (Stonechild and Waiser 1997, 221). Until the 1951 amendments to the Indian Act, it was illegal for Indigenous peoples to even protest the conditions of our own oppression, as raising money to fund court cases in the interest of protecting our basic human rights rendered us as criminals in our own homelands. In other words, when we attempted to address colonial intrusions, our efforts were criminalized. As was our very presence outside of reserve lands.

In the prairie west, the North West Mounted Police (NWMP) were charged with bringing Indigenous people, including the Métis, within the reach of Canadian law (Harring 1998, 242). Prior to the founding of the NWMP (which was later succeeded by the RCMP), the Hudson's Bay Company (HBC) exercised certain powers of law and governance yet infrequently interfered with Indigenous peoples' existing legal and political institutions (Harring 1998, 242). Early on in Indigenous-settler interactions, the NWMP are often described as maintaining relatively favorable relations with Indigenous peoples (particularly with certain groups such as the Blackfoot), taking an active role in restricting the presence of whisky traders and unwanted visitors within Indigenous communities. However, the 1885 Northwest Rebellion, among other events, resulted in the NWMP taking on a stronger role in the enforcement of policies geared towards Indigenous repression and assimilation (Stonechild and Waiser 1997).

While the mandate of the NWMP evolved over time, it played a central role in nation-building both by policing Indigenous people, and by creating a more inviting environment for prospective settlers who could be assured that they would be under the protection of Canadian law. And, in order to ensure that they could carry out these assurances, the NWMP were vested with extra-ordinary judicial power, leading scholars to describe the early NWMP as "a self-contained legal institution organized on a quasi-military model: Mounties arrested, prosecuted, judged, and jailed offenders under their jurisdiction" (Harring 1998, 241, cited in Starblanket 2019). The original form and operations of Canadian legal and political institutions were thus not only designed by and in the interest of protecting the territorially specific configurations of settler colonialism in Canada (Green 2017), they were authorized with the power to ensure the unilateral and comprehensive application of this "made-in-Canada" approach to maintaining law and order.

As time passed, early settlers sought new ways to provide for the stability of their settler societies. In the initial years of settlement, the "vanishing race" trope dominated settlers' perceptions of Indigenous peoples, and thus their concerns about the security of new settlements were directed to a greater extent towards the perceived invasion of 'their territories' by by subsequent waves of immigrants (known as 'new Canadians') who threatened the ethnic, religious, and linguistic composition of the prairies. Some scholars have attributed these sentiments to the success that white supremacist groups—such as the Orange Order and the Ku Klux Klan—found in the Saskatchewan region post World War II.[16] Over time, and as it became clear that the "vanishing Indian" trope would not in fact come to fruition, new policies had to be enacted to provide security against the "new Indian threat."

The exercise of law and order in the prairies, as Lesley Erickson notes, was a way for dominant groups to impose their vision of society, law, and morality on subordinate groups. Indeed, the settler construct "depended on the application of a system of law that was both discretionary and discriminatory" (2011, 19). The legal system placed primacy in the liberal individual citizen, protecting "his right to self-preservation and the pursuit of property [...] liberals envisaged the rights-bearing individual as the rational male, in opposition, they constructed women, indigenous peoples and the unpropertied as deficient individuals" (Erickson 2011, 22).

The contemporary experiences of both settlers and Indigenous peoples in the prairies should be contextualized by these histories. And it should come as no surprise that multiple contemporary inquiries into the interactions between Indigenous peoples and the criminal justice system have indicated that they continue to be marked by deeply rooted forms of Eurocentrism, racism, and sexism.[17] State institutions not only deprive Indigenous people of justice but operate to mask the frequent and extreme forms of violence that Indigenous people face when interacting with them. As the attitudes and operations engendered by these structures have been rendered normative over time, they are deemed completely "lawful" even when operating at a clear and continuous disadvantage to Indigenous peoples. In the process, the systemic racism that is embedded in the purportedly neutral and invisible backdrop of Canadian law is overlooked, as is the deeply rooted normalization of interpersonal racism within Canadian society that rationalizes the frequency of incidents of injustice and minimizes the perceived need for overhaul of the system. In many ways, we see the perfect distillation of this in not only the death of Colten Boushie and its immediate aftermath, but also in the trial of Gerald Stanley and his subsequent acquittal.

Far from transcending the violence of colonialism past, Canadian institutions still function to discipline and suppress Indigenous peoples and continue to provide protections for those who commit violence against them so long as it is rationalized by what we term (and describe in a later chapter as) "settler reason."

Designed by and for European newcomers who sought to institute their own legal orders in these lands, Canadian institutions of law and policing have since functioned as an integral part of the structure of settler colonialism in what is currently called Canada. The police, in particular, have been used to carry out much of the overt violence and forms of direct oppression committed against Indigenous people in the service of the national interest. As the institutional relationship between Indigenous, federal, and provincial governments has never been reconfigured in a way that deviates from these colonial origins, it should come as no surprise that the criminal justice system continues to operate in a way that reflects its earliest mandate.

Similar to the way in which the provision of "justice" unfolded surrounding the killing of Colten Boushie, examples of racial violence and discrimination within the Saskatchewan and broader Canadian criminal justice system abound. For example, in January 1991, Leo Lachance, a Cree trapper from Big River First Nation, went to the Prince Albert Northern Pawn and Gun Shop to potentially sell a few items. The pawn shop was a popular meeting space for prison guards and off-duty police officers and was owned and operated by Carney Milton Nerland, a known white supremacist and leader of the Jesus Christ Church of Aryan Nations in Saskatchewan. Soon after entering the shop LaChance was fatally shot by Nerland, his bullet propelled forward not only by his rifle, but also by centuries of settler colonial white supremacist hatred. Nerland was ultimately charged with manslaughter and given a 4-year sentence, of which he would only serve 2 years before being released on parole and placed in a witness protection program by the RCMP. What these incidents illustrate, and the plethora of cases like them (see: Pamela George, Tina Fontaine, among *many* others), is the asymmetrical treatment Indigenous peoples receive and are subjected to within the Canadian judicial system, relative to that of non-Indigenous peoples.[18]

Rather than regarding the Canadian legal system as something that has, from time to time, malfunctioned, we understand the legal system to be a mechanism that was designed for, and actively continues to carry out, the elimination of Indigenous people.

## *The System isn't Broken, it was Built This Way*

In our interactions with non-Indigenous institutions and populations, Indigenous peoples often find that matters of race and colonialism are deliberately left out of the picture, despite the undeniable existence of racial tensions and ongoing colonial dynamics on the prairies. Such was the case in the Stanley trial, where race relations were not mentioned once in the main trial proceedings, despite the rampant proliferation of settler stereotypes and assumptions about Indigenous peoples in the area. In the preliminary trial inquiry, witnesses were chided by the defense when they suggested that they had been subject to racist treatment by the RCMP, to the point where Judge Martel Popescul intervened in the defense's treatment of one of the Indigenous youth to say: "I'm concerned that [...] you've told her a number of times that—why you think that she shouldn't think that they're racist, that she continues to think that they are, and I'm not sure that we're going to get anywhere by continuing down this road" (*R. v. Stanley* 2017, 334).

Outside of the courts, Scott Spencer, Gerald Stanley's lawyer, took great pains to downplay the ways that racialized logics figured into Colten's death, suggesting that he did not want the trial to "become a referendum on race," and that he saw "no evidence that race played any part in the tragic circumstances that escalated on the Stanley Farm" (quoted in CBC News 2017).

Yet, the extreme racial tensions surrounding Boushie's death have been readily apparent throughout and following this case. Indeed, many commentators and reporters reproduced stereotypes and prejudices about Indigenous peoples, some of which are explicitly grounded on ideas of racial inferiority and deficiency, and others which use more coded language, such as associations between race and criminality, vagrancy, idleness, and alcohol/drug use. The irony here is that many were employing these explicitly or implicitly racialized ideas at the exact same moment that they were dismissing race as a relevant factor in Colten's death. It seemed that race was allowed to figure into the narrative when situating Indigenous people as perpetrators of crime, but when Indigenous people have been victims of crime, we are told that we shouldn't be playing the 'race card.'

The rhetoric of 'the race card' refers to the assumption that individuals who are trying to name or identify prejudice and discrimination are attempting to use their identity as a strategy to gain an advantage, or at the very least, that they are trying to bring the issue of race into contexts where it does not belong. Yet, the very notion of a 'race card' functions as a strategy to contain and discredit efforts to account for the implications of past and present experiences of racism (Edgar et al. 2019, 131).

In the prairies, negative perceptions of Indigenous people do not just emerge during the course of overtly racist interactions, but rather they form an unnamed and taken for granted social norm. Even as settler individuals in these spaces reproduce negative assumptions and representations of Indigenous people, they will often vehemently deny their own racism. When confronted about their race-based ideas, they can frequently be heard either refusing to admit that those views are racist, or conversely, explaining why they are *entitled* to hold and express these views. Regarding the latter, the explanations vary, but often they cite the fact that they live in a region with a high Indigenous population or work in a profession where they have to interact with many Indigenous people who have caused challenges for them. In other words, Indigenous people are to blame for the racism inflicted upon us and, in some cases, for the violence that it gives rise to.

The historical and present structures of racism and colonialism mark all interactions in the prairies; they do not only exist in select contexts. Racial tensions did not merely surface after Colten's death, but date back to the earliest interactions between Indigenous and non-Indigenous peoples in these spaces. We ask, then: how could the interactions between Gerald Stanley and the car of Indigenous youth on that farm be immune from these racialized associations? How could the Stanley family possibly be isolated from the dominant social, cultural, and political norms that mark prairie life? How could this incident be inoculated from the colonial story of the settlement of the prairie west?

Here there is a common dissociative tendency in contexts of colonialism, where there exists undeniable racialized hierarchies and patterns of discrimination that inform social interactions, yet law and politics are said to be immune from these influences.[19] Such was the case in Stanley's trial where the language of race rarely surfaced. Instead, the defense relied upon racialized associations between Indigeneity and deviance, troublemaking, and terror, and corresponding narratives of settler independence, industry, and lawfulness—without ever having to speak about race. It is precisely because these narratives are so deeply normalized in the prairies that they were able to make sense to the jury and, ultimately, help configure the outcome of the case.

The ongoing denial of settler colonialism and its racialized logics shapes popular representations of colonial histories as well as dominant understandings of Indigenous and non-Indigenous life in the prairies today. At a systemic level, narratives of colonial violence are often dismissed by settlers as a fabrication of historical revisionism while peaceful histories of colonial settlement and development are regarded as the 'correct,' 'unbiased,' or 'true' version of the past and present. Even when colonial violence is acknowledged (and it is rarely acknowledged in the prairies), it is situated as a historical phenomenon that is disconnected from contemporary contexts, which obscures the many ongoing operations of settler colonialism.

At an interpersonal level, the denial of racialized hierarchies blocks the potential for Indigenous suffering to be recognized and addressed, as Indigenous people are continually told that our lived experiences of oppression are a product of our own making, markings of a broken culture, an unwillingness to join Canadian society, or a product of gratuitous self-victimization and entitlement. At the same time, preconceived assumptions and stereotypes that many non-Indigenous people hold about Indigenous people and communities are rendered invisible. They are unremarkable because they have become the fabric of everyday life in the settler colonial context of Canada; indeed, these assumptions and stereotypes are informed by narratives of savagery, of deficiency, of deviancy that have been reproduced and reified for centuries, in the process becoming sedimented and normalized. To settlers in the prairies, then, Indigenous peoples have been and always will be this way, as this is the 'natural,' normative order of things, as told to them via the logics, imaginaries, and stories that settler colonialism and its proprietors cultivate.

Yet, despite what many Canadians would like to believe, the contemporary crises of relationship between Indigenous and non-Indigenous peoples in Canada do not exist in a vacuum. They cannot be divorced from the structures of colonialism and notions of racial hierarchy that both helped to produce, and are required to sustain, the Canadian state. This book, in many ways, is a response to Stanley's lawyer's assertion that the trial was not "a referendum on race," or to broader calls to leave race and its constitutive histories of colonialism 'out of the picture.' It is a purposeful effort to bring race and discrimination into focus, to adjust the aperture of the lens through which relations on the prairies are viewed (Dhillon 2017, 236).

This adjustment is necessary, as the narratives that we elaborate lay bare the discrepancies between settler colonial history and the tales Canada tells about itself. In many ways, these lies—of (white) civility and neutrality, of the inability to see race or the processes of colonization—are crucial to combat as they become the fodder for narratives that naturalize the deaths of Indigenous youth on the prairies. These narratives mark Indigenous deaths as personal, subjective problems, ones unmoored from history and politics and their effects. Yet, these are not individualized issues relevant only to the actors involved, but rather are a part of a longer history and structure of settler colonial violence, the scaffolding of which attempts to frame Stanley as an exceptional, yet justified, agent of violence, instead of positioning him as only one agent of violence in the longer history of force, coercion, and bodily harm enacted on Indigenous communities and their territories.

# 3

# *Whites "coveted Indian land but not land with Indians on it"* [20]

In the neighborhood gatherings of the men, and the visits of the women to each other's cabin, tales of peril with the Indians or of adventures in hunting the game which then abounded in the forests, were familiar, and often exciting subjects of conversation.

—James Barr Walker (1881)

The settler colonial imperative of land acquisition (and related processes of Indigenous elimination) on the prairies has several components.

The most immediate form of elimination is to physically remove Indigenous people from the land, encompassed in a variety of efforts geared towards what James Daschuk (2013) describes as "clearing the plains" of Indigenous peoples; the decimation of Indigenous food sources, the unmitigated spread of disease, and the failure to assist Indigenous populations were particularly prevalent strategies here. That is in addition to the reserve system, the pass system, residential schools, restrictions on traditional livelihoods, and other means of "clearing the way" for settlement that took place, and that continues to take place on the prairies.[21]

As discussed in chapter 2, the productive dimension of settler colonialism is that it does not replace Indigenous society in its entirety, but that what it replaces it with is a settler colonial society that maintains "the refractory imprint of the native counter-claim" (Wolfe 2006, 389). Thus, new settler identities have a tendency to "borrow" Indigenous motifs and symbols for the creation of their own cultural identity, in what Hunt terms "settler replacement narratives" that simultaneously appropriate symbols of Indigeneity while disavowing Indigenous peoples' active social and political existences and, indeed, our futures. (2018, 71-90).[22]

It is unsurprising, then, that Indigenous peoples, settler interactions with our governments, or responses to our resistance rarely appear in the literature on western political culture, and when they do, it is only marginally. If one had little knowledge of Canada, they could read many of the canonical works on regional politics and be left with the impression that western political culture formed entirely independently of interactions with Indigenous populations.

Yet, western political cultures cannot be adequately theorized independently as Indigenous peoples' ongoing political formations and expressions always shape the relationship as well. If settler society has to work to actively produce itself anew, it cannot do so without having to contend with the ongoing presence of Indigenous people and to find new ways to contain the ever-evolving 'Indian threat' to settler economies and livelihoods.[23]

In this context settler colonialism requires not just the establishment of settler societies, but also the establishment of new types of settler relationships with the land. In the prairies, as the region that was expected to produce resources for the rest of the country and for international export, settlers would be expected to use the land in a capacity that was seen to be more economically productive than Indigenous relations with these territories.

These justifications for colonization do not just emerge at the moment of contact, but also influence the ways in which settlers advance their own interests and dismiss Indigenous interests over time. In the contemporary context, one need only look at the countless comments online and on social media that denigrate Indigenous practices of stewardship and relationality with the living earth within conversations relating to resource management or exploitation in the prairies.

Conversely, Indigenous people who have been pro-development or pro-partnership throughout history have had a tendency to be depicted as the 'authoritative' Indigenous

GINA STARBLANKET & DALLAS HUNT

leadership whose legitimacy is presumed, and they are seen as those who should be trusted to make decisions for the 'rest of the Indians' who 'just don't get' how the proposals offered by Canada have been, and continue to be, in our best interest.

Returning to early settler life on the prairies, for the most part it has not lived up to the utopic trappings proliferated in dominant representations. While farming on the prairies has experienced short and intermittent periods of expansion and profitability over the years, it has also been accompanied by ongoing challenges. Access to highly fertile and affordable lands was not as seamless as depicted to prospective settlers, nor was farming these lands always as profitable as the campaigns had suggested.

As a result of the number of middlemen and high freight rates required to get their crops to markets, among other factors, the final prices of crops were often significantly lower than farmers desired. At a national level, four out of ten free homesteads failed between the years of 1870 to 1927, while in Saskatchewan 57% failed between 1911 to 1931 (Conway 2014, 40). From these and other dynamics emerged a number of particular concerns among many settlers in western Canada, including: a sense of alienation; questions surrounding the west's perceived role in Canadian confederation; critiques of large-scale capitalism, big business and financial interests; and chronic complaints surrounding central Canada's treatment of the west. Far from the promised land of prosperity, the west has been troubled by economic crises, volatility, anxieties, and uncertainties. Much of this is owed to the declining profitability of the agrarian economy and heavy dependence on the resource sector.

From 1931 onward, the farming population in the prairies has been outnumbered by the working class, yet populist political movements sought to create coalitions between these groups to combat big business and financial interests. Importantly, a common feature of these populist movements was the need to protect small-scale, private enterprises that would ensure that land remained "in the hands of the people." And as something that belongs in "the hands of the people," land has also become something that needs to be protected "by the hands of the people." Indeed, during the course of the trial, Stanley's lawyer argued he was "faced with intruders and didn't have the luxury to wait for police," with his seemingly remote location evoked to excuse vigilante-style violence as the most appropriate response to the presence of Indigenous bodies in 'non-Indigenous spaces.'

This sense of settlers' individual agency, authority, and sustainability also translates to other realms of life, such as the administration of law and governance. Indeed, there are a multiplicity of ways in which rural populations are called upon by one another to "take things into their own hands" (be it the economy, management of resources, labour, politics, policing). This contextualizes why farmers have also sought to take crime and justice into their own hands, which amplifies the sense of settler entitlement, and in fact their self-perceived right to "self-defense" to protect against Indigenous incursion into their lives and the lands they claim.

Prairie agrarian life has thus been marked by a strong perceived sense of self-sustainability and individualism, arising at least in part from the idea that farmers have weathered harsh, isolating conditions and have continually gotten through it with little government assistance. These dynamics also play into the hostility and resentment that many prairie settlers hold towards Indigenous people, and towards what they perceive to be Indigenous calls for 'special treatment' by the national government. These hostilities are also amplified in the prairies as a result of popular misconceptions surrounding the distinct nature of Indigenous peoples' political relationships with the national government, not least of which involves a failure to properly comprehend the nature and contemporary implications of the numbered treaties.

As discussed in Chapter 2, it is important to be mindful of the distinct relationships between colonial states and the types of commodities they seek to access and exploit. In contexts of settler colonialism, the primary commodity is the land. However, not all populations across the various regions of Canada find their livelihoods so intimately dependent upon unthreatened ownership of vast tracts of landscape as do farmers.

In the prairies there is a high rural population. Given the particular economies here, a significant population depends on access to, and security of, land for their livelihood. Statistics Canada observes that "nearly all farmland today is managed by people with white settler ancestry," and material dominance is a central aspect of white settler farmer identity (Statistics Canada

2011, cited in Rotz 2017). To maintain this domination over time, settlers deploy particular logics toward Indigenous peoples that seek to ensure that once removed, Indigenous peoples are categorized in a variety of ways to ensure they are kept away from these settler-lands (Wolfe 2016, 10).

Farmers have played a distinct role in the creation of settler colonial societies. The freedom and industry—indeed their existence and livelihood—sought in settler colonies was directly dependent on their ability to use vast tracts of land, which depended (and still depends) upon the dispossession of Indigenous people. And as the socio-political climate has shifted over the years in ways that have increasingly acknowledged that the processes of genocide committed against Indigenous people were wrong (though, of course, this is not acknowledged in all instances), Indigenous peoples' rights and claims to territory have found themselves pitted against those whose livelihoods depend upon our dispossession and subordination.

While the myth of the 'vanishing Indian' was popular during the early phases of colonial settlement, when the numbers of Indigenous people were still declining as a result of disease, starvation, and violence, the population of Indigenous peoples in the prairies has only grown since the early $20^{th}$ century. Yet, despite (or perhaps because of) the clear failure of policies geared towards 'clearing the plains' of Indigenous people in our entirety, the eliminatory logics of settler colonialism continued to manifest in different ways. Wolfe points to the distinct forms of racialization that occur in response to territorial engulfment, that is, the "crisis occasioned when colonizers are threatened with the requirement to share social space with the colonized" (2016, 14). This occurs in the wake of the frontier, when Indigenous peoples become physically contained within settler societies. In such cases, the obstruction that Indigenous people present to the development of settler society is no longer merely physical, but remains present in the set of alternative sovereignties that Indigenous peoples represent and assert (A. Simpson, 2016; L. Simpson, 2017; Wolfe, 2006).

The form of sovereignty that can provide settler populations with the security they so desperately desire is always prevented by Indigenous peoples' counter claim to these same lands. As this counter claim becomes increasingly recognized as legitimate, and in fact gains political traction precisely because of the ways that Indigenous rights have been ignored throughout history, settler populations need to continually reinforce a range of stereotypes and assumptions to dismiss and delegitimize Indigenous voices. These include the assumptions that Indigenous people are deficient because they refuse or 'fail' to assimilate and the construction of Indigenous deviance through tactics like criminalization, pathologization, and other strategies that render Indigenous people as dangerous anomalies in our own lands. These processes of externalization are particularly amplified in the prairies because of the ways in which histories of populism and collectivism have associated security and prosperity with the notion of uniformity, community, and togetherness, which either situates Indigenous peoples as requiring assimilation into the settler society or as inevitably external to it.

That the narrative of the 'vanishing Indian' was very obviously an incorrect one—proven by the growth of Indigenous populations in the prairies—allowed for a complementary narrative to emerge: that of the heroic adventurer who managed to survive against the remaining 'Indian threat' in the outposts of Empire. The depiction of Indigenous populations as savage, unruly, uncivilized people did more than bolster settlers' sense of superiority and entitlement; it also constructed a narrative of violent, bloodthirsty, irrational Indians who, left to their own devices, were sure to engage in unprovoked violence against settlers.

From these early renderings of Indigeneity *as* deviance, Indigenous people emerged as the primary perceived threat to the settler state and social order. As Joanne Barker has argued, narratives of Indigeneity and terrorism are continuously co-produced in contexts of colonialism, and serve a crucial political function in the establishment and continuity of empire, as well as the containment of Indigenous political mobilization. As Indigenous peoples necessarily represent a threat to the empire's sense of security, their suppression then represents the means through which the order of whiteness is sustained.[24]

Barker explains that affective terror is a necessary condition of the state structure, which must justify both settler power and privilege by framing Indigenous exercises of power as a threat. Enter the figure of the "murderable Indian," which situates Indigenous people as subjects that settlers can and should anticipate harm from, and thus, justifies the need for settlers to protect themselves against at any cost. Indeed, Lisa Ford writes about the use of 'tales of peril' among settlers to justify the legality of the lawless acts that they have committed against Indigenous peoples. These tales, which represent a series of carefully crafted and often repeated narratives, have been employed by settlers in colonial contexts since the late 1700s to justify violence against Indigenous people and, in some cases, their murder. Ford explains that, despite the illegality of murder, there were a number of 'normative exceptions' to justify killing an Indigenous person, including claims to self-defense, provocation, and defense of property. As a means of protecting against Indigenous intrusion, the murder of Indigenous people was seen as integral to settler survival, particularly in less populous regions. Ford writes that "by assuring law officers that Indigenous wrongs provoked settler violence, killers asserted effectively that their actions were both legal and justifiable" (2011, 101).

In one instance that bears a striking resemblance to the Stanley case, Ford cites an 1822 case from colonial Australia, where a man named Seth Hawker was acquitted of murdering an Indigenous woman in an Illawarra cornfield. Much like the Stanley defense, she notes that personal peril, Indigenous culpability, and provocation infused "every aspect of the inquiry" (2011, 101). Unsurprisingly, the narrative that was constructed in the courtroom followed a similar logic to that used in the Stanley case, focusing on the 'troublesome' and 'treacherous' nature of the "local Aborigines" and asking witnesses if "the Aborigines" had been warned of the consequences of thieving (102). To be clear, the use of peril as a justification for murder was employed flexibly to include the defense of one's own life or property. Ford also notes how such normative exceptions to the law were made possible through settlers "control of legal discourse, legal evidence, and juries" which, taken together, would ensure that the common law "served the interests of plurality" (86). Beyond the Hawker case, Ford cites a number of instances where similar logics of settler peril and Indigenous provocation were used across colonial contexts in order to normalize the violence and deaths of Indigenous peoples, but also to frame these deaths as a result of Indigenous culpability, deviance, and the inherent threat that they posed to settler life and property (103).

In the Canadian prairies, settlers mobilize demarcations of territory, property, citizenship, and national identity in order to affirm their own superiority and authority by way of contrast with Indigenous peoples. This involves processes of racializing, gendering, and othering Indigenous peoples that ultimately create protections around the normative, white, settler order while simultaneously subordinating Indigenous peoples. This order is co-constituted by the Canadian legal system, which in turn justifies the criminalization and attempted elimination of Indigenous peoples. As Erickson writes, "the law constituted race, class, and gender in colonial settings" which, in turn, crystallized divisions that shaped trial outcomes (2011, 18). Furthermore, because the courts were so intimately connected to the institutional structure of the settler state, the legal system was intentionally designed to naturalize and ensure the reproduction of Canadian sovereignty over Indigenous lands and peoples.

The contemporary configurations of Canadian institutions must be contextualized and understood in light of these origins and their continuities. For they are not merely historical phenomena, but remain woven into the fabric of Canadian social, political, and legal life. As Barker emphasizes, so affective were representations and associations of terror in colonial contexts that Indigenous peoples are always already positioned as terrorists, or as inherent threats to the interests of the nation and its proper, rights-bearing citizens. Indeed, in the contemporary context, we see these associations between Indigenous peoples and domestic terrorism being reinvigorated, especially in the context of blockades and other forms of resistance against resource development projects that are said to serve the 'national interest.'[25] Thus Indigenous people who seek to carry out our responsibilities to the land are repeatedly framed as 'radical activists' undertaking illegal actions. This framing pits even the most modest assertions of Aboriginal or treaty rights as being contrary to the 'national interest,' which in turn justifies, normalizes, and/or conceals state violence against Indigenous peoples.

This framing is part of a common settler story told about Indigenous peoples in the prairies. The story assumes that whenever Indigenous peoples raise concerns—have 'issues'—or make claims to rights, they will undoubtedly take away from 'real

Canadian issues,' or rights. In this way, the national interest—
that is 'real Canadian issues/rights'—has always depended on
the denial of Indigenous peoples' rights. It's presumed that both
sets of rights cannot and should not exist simultaneously or are
not conjoined.

The assumption that important political conversations
are being hijacked by meaningless tropes and demands—that
Canada's proper political interests are being threatened by oppo-
nents of the 'national interest' (read: Indigenous people)—is
an incredibly common one in the prairies. The thinking is that
Indigenous people cannot possibly represent legitimate political actors unless we are agreeing to proposals from Canadian
governments or industry (assimilatory offerings, modern treaty-
making, development proposals, self-government agreements).
Conversely, those who resist such offerings are rarely recognized
as enacting a political critique, but rather are instead always
nefarious troublemakers who hold the potential to derail movements towards economic prosperity and social order. Such narratives, in turn, justify the use of violence and force in removing
Indigenous people from our homelands.[26]

Canadian society was built upon Indigenous dispossession
and legal/political subordination, but it also has to be continually
maintained and rendered "secure" from new threats to its legitimacy. For the prairies to truly represent a white, settler geography, Indigenous removal and suppression has to be actively
carried out in perpetuity. Sunera Thobani observes how the
'Indigenous threat' is often cast as 'the outsider' or 'the stranger'

who "'wants' what nationals have;" indeed, such individuals are deemed a threat as they are "defined as devoid of the qualities and values of the nation—as being quite alien to these" (2007, 4). As a consequence, the "stranger provokes anxiety, if not outright hostility. Indeed, the stranger has historically been suspected of embodying the potential for the very negation of nationality within modernity" (2007, 4).

Regardless of whether the language of race was used in the Stanley trial (this, after all, was not a "referendum on race"), these associations remain intact. Thus, given these tendencies, it should come as no surprise that when Gerald Stanley's defence lawyer Scott Spencer attempted to contextualize the killing of Colten Boushie, he argued that Stanley was defending his land from intrusion, stating that, for farmers, "your yard is your castle:"

> This is really not a murder case at all. This is a case about what can go terribly wrong when you create a situation which is really in the nature of a home invasion. For farm people, your yard is your castle. And that's part of the story here, and you've heard a lot of the evidence... But that's what we have here is we have a family. And Gerry—Gerry didn't go looking for trouble on August 9th, 2016. He was doing what he does every day. He was working on his ranch. And that's what they were all doing. They were working on the ranch, cutting the grass. The son comes home, he gets put to work. I don't even think he got put to work, just naturally went to work. That's what the day started like for Gerry and the Stanleys. But what happened is they faced essentially intruders. And we can debate about what the intention of some or all of

the—the young people were. And they were—they were young people, not kids, but—but young people that came to the yard that day. But you have to view it from Gerry's perspective, what he felt, what he thought when he was faced with this sudden intrusion. The fear of the unknown. Really, in the—really, in the—the nature of—of being terrorized. (*R. v. Stanley* 2018, 607)

Note the language used in this quote. Gerry "didn't go looking for trouble" stands in contrast to the implication that the Indigenous youth were spending their day "up to no good" or "looking for trouble," phrasing which lends itself to the idea that 'they got what they were asking for.' Further, the phrase "what we have here is we have a family" stands in contrast to the de-humanized representations of Colten and his friends that surrounded this trial, who were represented as "intruders" or the architects of "misadventure," and whose own family and community relations are either irrelevant or unimportant.

Then, there is the language of industriousness and productiveness used to describe Sheldon Stanley, the diligent son who came home and "naturally went to work" on the ranch. Contrast this to the language used to describe the Indigenous youth—they were to be viewed as "young people," not sons and daughters, kids, or even youth (even though at least one of them was a minor). Meanwhile 28-year-old Sheldon Stanley was rarely referred to as an adult but was described as Gerald Stanley's son 29 times throughout the trial. What is being manufactured here is a story that mirrors the posters described at the outset of the book, one that centers a nuclear settler family hard at work on their farm, and legitimizes violence against Indigenous youth in their ancestral territories.

Indeed, the quote from Spencer above reproduces many of the narratives Canada has invoked, since its origins, to frame idealized representations of prairie settler life. Sarah Carter writes that "[t]he job of empire building was man's work," and that "the white British male settler or frontiersman was the heroic figure, taming the wild frontier into productivity and profitability" (2016, 7). In a prairie context and at "the heart of this mythic construction of empire is the farm—a cultivated, constructed site of agriculture, of nature improved by the intervention of 'man' that functioned as both the material impress and reproducing sign of empire" (Casid 2005, xxii).

What should not be lost here is how castles (and now farms) have served as sites of capitalist accumulation and protectionism, as romanticized spaces wherein heroic kings protect against incursion from hostile outside forces. Like a modern-day King Arthur or Lancelot, Stanley believed he needed to not only protect his kingdom, but he also rationalized his actions as driven by the need to save his 'maiden,' his wife, who he claimed was out of sight at the time of the shooting. Indeed, it is not a stretch to say that Stanley, along with the other out-spoken farmers in the Saskatchewan farming community advocating for violence, have been represented historically and in the present day as heroic frontiersmen taming the wild and cultivating their little outposts of empire. All of this is to say that we've seen this rhetoric and imagery before, making it clear that colonial legacies directly shape contemporary relationships. For Stanley's defenders, however, this story is disconnected from the processes of marginalization, of subordination and of othering cultural difference that have served to justify and in some cases, legally entrench, Indigenous erasure and elimination in Canada's collective interest.

While the Stanley defense asked people on the prairies to imagine themselves in "Gerry's boots," nobody is asking them to put themselves in the shoes of those whose lives and homelands have to be continually subjugated in order for this imagery of "the castle" to be sustained. Castles evoke mental portraits of fortresses besieged, of hordes of enemies attempting to crash the gates of the wealthy, aristocratic, and ultimately armed gentry defending themselves against the blood-thirsty intruders outside their walls and beyond their moats. These, no doubt, are the images and representations Spencer hoped to cultivate in the minds of those sympathetic to or willing to entertain the idea of Stanley's innocence or his justification for the use of deadly force. While Stanley's social and economic location, and his experience, intentions, beliefs, and aspirations all formed part of the narrative that shaped the outcome of this trial, the particular experiences of Indigenous peoples vis-à-vis the police and legal system were deemed irrelevant.

But what if we invert the intruder narrative? What if we bear in mind that the continuity of settler presence on Indigenous lands is itself premised on intrusion, a constant structure of intrusion dependent upon Indigenous disappearance? How can we reconcile the inhospitable notion of "intrusion" that then rationalizes settler violence with the nearly inconceivable acts of generosity that Indigenous peoples have extended and continue to extend in agreeing to share the land through treaty? Viewed from this perspective, the settler imaginary of a constant threat of Indigenous violence appears as a perverse reversal of the actual colonial reality: that Indigenous existence itself is understood by settlers as a threat that always already rationalizes the use of violence.

## *Not Just a Glitch in the System*

Many condemned the acquittal of Stanley as another stark failure of the legal system to provide justice for Indigenous people. While it's true there was no justice for Colten, to characterize the outcome as a failure or deficiency of the system is a misleading and damaging understatement. It implies the outcome was a functional error, premised on the assumption that the Canadian legal system has the inherent capacity to provide justice to Indigenous people in the same neutral and fair manner it does for settlers. Yet the belief in equality before and under the law, the notion that one will receive a neutral and fair experience when interacting with the justice system, is not one that Indigenous peoples in Canada can readily count upon.

Even if a system or policy claims to treat all citizens equally, or to operate through a neutral, objective process, all people are not equal in our socio-political positions and thus the impacts of the system are differently experienced. The notion that the Stanley decision was a mere 'failure in justice' overlooks the ways in which the Canadian policing and legal systems have more often than not served as the primary instruments used to authorize and carry out violence committed against Indigenous peoples in Canada, past and present. Further, it overlooks the ways in which the security and protection desired by mainstream Canadians is often achieved at the expense of Indigenous interests and well-being, including our legal and political rights.

This occurs in the everyday, interpersonal interactions that Indigenous people have with the police; the examples are endless and already known to many Indigenous people even if they are dismissed by the general population. One of the manifestations of the unequal administration of justice is that Indigenous peoples' claims are often under-investigated or not taken seriously (the case of Robert Pickton and Murdered and Missing Indigenous Women, Girls, and Two-Spirit peoples being just one of several examples). Many narratives about Indigenous people shape these interactions, leading the police to cast missing Indigenous women, girls, and Two-Spirit peoples as likely just succumbing to the inevitable consequences of their perceived lifestyle.[27]

In other cases, the police have been directly responsible for physical violence, sexual assault and in some instances the death of Indigenous people in custody. For instance, Saskatchewan is still haunted by the infamous Starlight tours, whereby police officers would (and may still) drive Indigenous peoples to the outskirts of city limits in freezing temperatures to leave them there to walk back into cities/towns. Some freeze to death in the process. This horrific violence is often said to have been occurring for 40-50 years, with the first *documented* instance happening in 1976 when a Saskatoon police officer was disciplined for taking an Indigenous woman to "the outskirts of the city and abandoning her there" (*Windspeaker*, 2003; Green, 2006).

At a broader level, we see the RCMP, bolstered by the Canadian legal system, physically assaulting and displacing Indigenous people from our traditional territories for protecting our rights, and labelling us as "terrorists" in the process. These processes, which is to say the (quasi)-military deployment of Canadian police forces in response to Indigenous communities protecting their territories, has many manifestations: Oka, Elsipogtog, Unist'ot'en, to name only a few. The effect, however, remains the same: Indigenous peoples are criminalized and brutalized for making assertions to their homelands and their right to protect them. In contrast, Gerald Stanley was able to use extra-judicial force to make a claim to what he perceived to be his property, his territory, and exercised his petty sovereignty with impunity.[28]

And even in the face of countless inquiries into Indigenous peoples' interactions with the Canadian legal system that have identified issues of systemic racism and discrimination, many commentators are quick to diagnose the failures of the legal system as isolated issues, or the actions of a few extreme individuals who have abused their power and authority. The proposed remedies are now all too familiar: cultural awareness training, the hiring of more Indigenous people in these institutions, and maybe, if one is *very* lucky, an apology or admission of wrongdoing, and a commitment to 'do better.' This, obviously, is not enough, and the Indigenous activists, artists, and communities drawing attention to these manifestations of settler violence remain unacknowledged, unaddressed, and unheard.

# 4

# "Settler Reason" and the Unheard

When we look back to the past we do not see where the Cree nation has ever watered the ground with the white man's blood, he has always been our friend and we his [...].

—Tee-tee-quay-say (quoted in Morris 1880, 215)

... the Natives who have survived the initial catastrophe of invasion and violent dispossession—you can't just carry on shooting them on sight. It doesn't work for the settler rule of law that has to appear to be conducted fairly and legitimately.

—Patrick Wolfe (Kauanui and Wolfe 2012, 241)

While colonialism, racism, sexism, transphobia, and homophobia play out in distinctive ways in different places, the prairies are home to a particular brand of racism, xenophobia, and denial of contemporary colonialism that all-too-often betrays the possibility of existing in healthy relationships.

Consider a 2014 poll on discrimination that assessed comfort levels between cultural groups across Canada. Respondents of different ages, races, genders, and geographical locations were asked to gauge their own comfort levels with respect to a number of scenarios that would require them to engage with Indigenous peoples. There were no differences between age groups or gender, but there were significant regional variations; respondents from Alberta, Manitoba, and Saskatchewan expressed discernably lower comfort levels with respect to engaging with Indigenous peoples (Levasseur, 2014).

As well, a 2016 poll conducted by the Environics Institute entitled *Canadian Public Opinion on Aboriginal Peoples* revealed that negative attitudes towards Indigenous peoples were highest in Alberta, Manitoba, and Saskatchewan—the provinces with the highest proportion of Indigenous people relative to the overall population.[29]

This latter poll identified five distinct groups or segments of non-Indigenous Canadians. While it is beyond the purview of this book to engage with each segment, one of them—the aptly named 'dismissive naysayers' segment—is of particular interest. Analysis of the poll results revealed that dismissive naysayers were most likely to be male, older, were the least urbanized of all groups, and tended to live in smaller towns and rural areas. This is the group that stood out as having the most negative views of Indigenous peoples, and could be distinguished as those who placed the least importance on Indigenous history and culture, were the least likely to see socio-economic disparity between Indigenous peoples and other Canadians, and were the most likely to see Indigenous peoples as being responsible for their own problems. This is also the segment that was most heavily concentrated in the prairie provinces.

The prairies generally had the highest rates of respondents who disagreed that Indigenous peoples have unique rights (2016, 14), strongly agreed that Indigenous peoples have a "sense of entitlement," and were more likely to see Indigenous peoples themselves as "the main obstacle to achieving social and economic equality" (2016, 23). Respondents in Saskatchewan were also some of the least likely to acknowledge that Indigenous peoples experience frequent discrimination (2016, 27).

While the purpose of this poll was to uncover public opinion about Indigenous people across Canada, it also speaks to more than mere opinion. For the stories that people hold as true—whether these are the stories that underlie the settler 'good life' in the prairies, or the stories that settlers tell about Indigenous people in the prairies—represent an interpretive frame that shapes how individuals experience and make sense of the world around them.[30]

While the Crown, the defense, and the judge focused on putting forward the available evidence in the Stanley trial and instructing the jury to draw facts from the evidence, we are interested in drawing out the filter through which they made sense of these facts, a lens that is made up of the less tangible yet highly influential stories, assumptions, and associations that shadow the 'presentation of facts.'

'Facts' are not objective pieces of data that hold one singular truth; rather they are given meaning and understood through the norms, values, and perceptions of those who hold the power to interpret and adjudicate them. When Indigenous people try to name this filter, we are told to leave 'history' or 'race' (read: colonialism) out of the picture, denying the many ongoing ways in which settler colonial values and systems have shaped, and continue to shape, life in the prairies today. We are charged with 'pushing an agenda' when we critically deconstruct or attempt to circumvent this filter. The Boushie family realized this from the outset and petitioned for an out-of-province prosecutor to try the Stanley case. This move was driven by the desire to see a fair trial, which they knew could not be found in a region with a well-documented and continuous legacy of racism and colonialism.

In fact, the mere suggestion that Stanley *should* be held accountable for the death of Colten Boushie sparked outrage from the surrounding rural population, evidencing further the level of white entitlement that settlers hold in these structurally racist spaces. Concomitantly, the fact that the Boushie family, and Indigenous people more generally, expressed distrust towards the Canadian legal system, was also cause for frustration among settlers, as many perceived the system as working in a fair and impartial way. The public response to this case shows just how delicate the settler story is, but also how aggressively and doggedly Stanley's peers and supporters have sought to guard it.

Indeed, the assertion that the Canadian justice system "can do better," as articulated by then Justice Minister Jody Wilson-Raybould in the aftermath of Stanley's acquittal, also sparked an outcry from a large swath of the Canadian public.

An access to information request to Public Safety Canada revealed a subsequent onslaught of e-mails from the Canadian public that condemned Wilson-Raybould for her comments, while others criticized Wilson-Raybould for commenting on the trial, concerned that her comments might undermine the public's confidence in the legal process. (As though Indigenous peoples' confidence in said system wasn't already undermined—historically and in present day.) And still others petitioned for the national government to craft a plan to provide for the "poor helpless farmers" who reside "in isolated situations" and "who feel threatened and [whose] property rights [are] disrespected." All of this is to say that even rhetorical political statements face public resistance for their possible encroachment on white settler entitlement and affirmation of the violence committed against Indigenous peoples.

Such outrage stems from the fact that Indigenous peoples are being *seen* in this moment, even if it is fleeting, and this in turn bequeaths a sense of humanity to Indigenous peoples. And if Indigenous peoples are not only seen, but humanized, it might be more difficult to eliminate us, both symbolically and bodily, in the present and future. And it may make it difficult for settlers to reconcile themselves to the fact that their ancestors and they themselves are complicit in these ongoing acts of elision, erasure, and elimination.

Another common strategy used to dismiss Indigenous peoples' accounts of racism and colonialism is to situate these as past phenomena divorced from contemporary realities (Coulthard, 2014). The notion that the past is disconnected from the present serves to minimize the association between racism, colonialism, and violence against Indigenous people, situating these instead as products of Indigenous peoples' own creation.

This blocks the potential for recognizing the harms faced by Indigenous peoples (such as those experienced by Colten, his friends, and relatives) to be acknowledged and addressed, as we are continually told that our lived experience is a fabrication of our own doing or not believable. Even when harms are recognized in mainstream discourses, Indigenous accounts of violence are regularly divorced from racial politics and the violences of settler colonial history.

In a region with such deep colonial and racialized divisions, what was deemed a 'fair trial' for Stanley came at the expense of a trial that could have enabled something resembling justice for Colten and his family. Stanley's defense team constructed a narrative that clearly resonated and held traction with the all-white jury. The narrative was consistent with their inherited, settler colonial interpretive frame, and did not allow the possibility for an alternate framing, complete with the (Indigenous) contexts and stories that would inform it. While the Crown prosecutors made some effort to challenge elements of the defense's narrative, the voices and experiences of the Boushie family remained largely unheard. As was any account of the socio-political context in which Colten's killing occurred.

Recently, there have been some minor attempts to consider the role of systemic colonial violence and enduring asymmetrical relations when addressing incidents of violence against Indigenous peoples.

For example, in the judgement in *R. v. Barton* (2019), Justice Michael J. Moldaver explained the appropriate steps that a trial judge should take to ensure that the jury is aware of contexts of colonialism and self-reflexive of their own racial biases. In particular, when instructing a jury he said:

In my view, trial judges should be given discretion to tailor the instruction to the particular circumstances, preferably after having consulted with the Crown and the defense. In a case like the present, the trial judge might consider explaining to the jury that Indigenous people in Canada—and in particular Indigenous women and girls—have been subjected to a long history of colonization and systemic racism, the effects of which continue to be felt (*R. v. Barton* 2019, 201)

Prior to this, Justice Moldaver indicated:

[t]rial judges, as gatekeepers, play an important role in keeping biases, prejudices, and stereotypes out of the courtroom. In this regard, one of

the main tools trial judges have at their disposal is the ability to provide instructions to the jury... such instructions can in my view play a role in exposing biases, prejudices, and stereotypes and encouraging jurors to discharge their duties fairly and impartially (2019, 197).

These instructions from *Barton* are markedly different from the instructions given by Judge Martel Popescul in the Stanley trial:

You must consider the evidence and make your decision on a *rational* and fair consideration of all the evidence, and not on passion or sympathy or prejudice against the accused, the Crown, or anyone else connected with the case. In addition, you must not be influenced by public opinion. Your duty as jurors is to assess the evidence impartially. (*R. v. Stanley* 2018, 879)

Judge Popescul did not direct the jury to be attentive to the very narratives and material realities that produced the conditions that instigated the confrontation between Stanley and the Indigenous youth, and which led to the tragic killing of Colten—the history of settler colonialism, Indigenous dispossession, and continual violence against Indigenous bodies.

Thus, in a transparent effort to ensure that the Stanley case at least appeared to consist of an objective process, matters of colonialism were not named at all during the trial, while matters of race only surfaced marginally.

Yet the absence of any significant mention of race, in a legal proceeding that serves as a microcosm of the region, characterized as it is by a long legacy of race-based divisiveness, is troubling to say the least.

While the court directed the jury not to pay attention to the media, the internet, or newspapers, the reality is that an all-white jury from this region didn't need to watch the news or surf the internet to have their opinions of Indigenous people negatively influenced.

These racialized logics are already sewn into the fabric of the socio-political environment in which they reside.

Yet, this issue was never confronted as their impartiality, prudence, and reason were presumed to accompany their whiteness. Not only this, but prospective Indigenous jury members were summarily ruled out by Stanley's attorney through peremptory challenges, presumably because they were assumed to lack the objective, impartial reasoning that an all-white jury purportedly has. In this instance, then, while the jurors were encouraged not to pay attention to media because of the potential racial tensions the media may have stoked, the *very composition* of the jury was constituted by racial judgements.

White settlers have the privilege of being given the benefit of the doubt when it comes to their credibility, neutrality, responsibility, and reasonableness. At the same time Indigenous people are presumed to have negative intentions, be deceptive, unreliable, and threatening. As the adjudicators of "reason," the jury interprets the information in front of them through their own frame of reference surrounding what good, or at least 'reasonable,' behaviour looks like. The frame is informed by, and works to reproduce, colonial and racial narratives that are deeply embedded in the prairies.

## "Settler Reason" and its Co-Constitutive Others

As part of the court's charge to the jury, Justice Popescul directed jurors to focus on the question of whether Stanley's actions were a blatant deviation from the level of care in handling a firearm that a "reasonable person" would employ in the same circumstances.

The questions then become, what is considered "reasonable" by an all-white jury from the Battlefords judicial district, and is the understanding of "reason" they privilege and prioritize going to be visibly different from what would be considered reasonable by an Indigenous person?

Stanley's levels of "reason" or unreason in a high-crisis situation are not challenged in a significant way or open to debate throughout the trial. Rather he is assumed to be in possession of a form of "reason" at all times. This, of course, differs from the level of "reason" attributed to or projected onto Colten and his friends that day; they were undoubtedly thought to be lacking "reason" (in many ways evinced by them daring to be on the farm at all).

In delivering his hour and a half long charge to the jury, not once did the judge offer any context surrounding why the Indigenous youth, some of whom had just witnessed their friend killed in front of them (and one of whom was forced into the back of a police car and taken on a high-speed chase), might not trust the police enough to provide their version of events. Justice Popescul did not explicitly tell the jury that they should believe Stanley over the youth, but issued directives such as "use your collective common sense to decide whether the witnesses know what they are talking about and whether they are telling the truth" (*R. v. Stanley* 2018, 881).

Additionally, he offered little context surrounding the substantially different relationships with law enforcement that led to Stanley having what the judge would describe as "friendly," "relaxed," and "cordial" communications with investigators (Roach 2019, 73), in contrast to the experience that the Indigenous youth had communicating with the investigators—an experience framed by the pre-existing experiences that Indigenous people have towards the legal system and its officials in the prairies. As one of the youth, Belinda Jackson, indicated in her preliminary testimony: "You can't really expect me to be truthful with these police that are like racist and thinking that I was on that farm to steal [...] I really didn't know what to say [...] I was scared. I was in shock" (*R. v. Stanley* 2017, 329).

Despite the fact that some of the youth had just witnessed their friend killed in front of them, the Crown prosecutor did not call a trauma expert as a witness; a trauma expert may have explained the memory patterns of individuals who have suffered a traumatic event, or contextualized how the testimonies of trauma victims should be interpreted. And, it should come as no surprise that a middle-aged, white farmer, who resided in the same region as many of the jurors, would come to better reflect the criteria informing the jury's interpretation of "credibility" than a group of Indigenous youth would (*R. v. Stanley* 2018, 841). We also want to note that the defense used incredibly paternalistic language when referencing the youths' testimony, referring to the youths' statements as "a little cute," or prefacing their testimony with "it was kind of cute that [...]" (*R. v. Stanley* 2018, 841-842). These sorts of framings mirror paternalistic and colonial representations of Indigenous people that have been reproduced throughout the history of settler-Indigenous interactions. They are merely one part (among many others employed in this case) of what Jakeet Singh (2004) refers to as the 'language games' that emerge from a particular history and inform the actions and identities of particular groups of people. These language games undoubtedly would have informed the jury's assessment of what constituted credibility and, moreover, what constituted reasonable conduct.

References to the behaviors of the Indigenous youth (both presumed and actual), unaccompanied by any relevant context, were often employed to bolster these notions of "settler reason" and the Indigenous youths' lack of "reason." Ultimately, the outcome of the trial hinged on what would ultimately be considered "reasonable conduct" by Stanley towards a collective of "unreasonable" Indigenous youth, and how this would appear to the group of settlers who made up the jury. These questions, of course, are steeped in the stories and collective histories that the jurors bring to the case, including colonial narratives about Indigenous people as intentionally threatening and inherently untrustworthy.

Sylvia Wynter diagnoses what we call "settler reason" as a product of the Eurocentric and western construction of "Man," a figure who is always already accorded a subject-hood/humanity because he embodies the "white, Western, bourgeois conception of the human" (2003, 260). Man, then, is always presumed to be rational, and is constituted by his opposite, the "irrational/subrational Human Other to [his] civic-humanist, rational self-conception" (281-2).

This "rational self-conception" is applied broadly to all settler populations in what is currently called Canada, and excludes Indigenous and other racialized peoples, usually to their detriment. In this way, on the day of Colten's murder he and his friends were not only excluded from the category of reason—and thus, in many ways barred from the category of humanity—but were also subsequently barred from it in the courtroom as well; as were any and all Indigenous peoples that might—but ultimately didn't—sit as a juror.

The Stanley case would come to be defined by a notion of settler reason that could be deployed in juridical and everyday contexts, and could be mobilized to not only rationalize the killing of brown bodies, but also to absolve Stanley from the violence he committed.

That "reason" is framed in such a troubling way throughout this whole case is evidence of how "settler reason" operates:

certain bodies—predominantly white, male, middle-to-upper class bodies—are said to possess reason, while other bodies are excluded from this category entirely. Beyond this, if one is not in possession of this "settler reason," or if they transgress it, they are immediately susceptible to sanctioned violence. This is why it is *reasonable* for Stanley to shoot an unarmed, young Cree man in the back of the head, and to do so with impunity—that is, to be eventually acquitted.

The expectation placed on Colten and his friends is that they should have catered their desires, actions, and movements to this settler reason. Having failed to do so, and having entered farm lands that do not 'belong' to them, it is understood as only *reasonable* that they should expect to be shot or shot at. Here, no room is accorded to the idea that maybe *it is reasonable* for Colten and his friends to traverse and travel on their ancestral territories; that this is something that their ancestors have been doing for centuries. Indeed, settler colonial mythologies suggest that when Indigenous peoples enter these spaces of settler reason (forts, castles, camps, etc.), they do so only to do harm, and thus should enter them at their own peril.

But what if we interpreted the interactions surrounding Colten's death through a different frame of reference, such as the intended nature of the treaty relationship? For Indigenous people in the prairies, treaties are central agreements that govern our relationship with colonial governments and with non-Indigenous people in Canada.[31] They are viewed as having as much force today as when they were originally signed, and remain absolutely crucial to understanding settler-Indigenous responsibilities to one another.

## Encountering Strangers

In negotiating Treaty 6, Indigenous leaders sought to enter into relations of care and assistance between parties. They sought guarantees for the ongoing ability to enact our existing ways of life while acquiring new knowledge and skills, particularly ones relating to agriculture that would be crucial for their livelihood (Taylor, 1985). They asked for medicines to be supplied, and for assistance in times of famine and pestilence so that future generations would have an adequate quality of life in the face of hardship (Opekokew, 1992). They committed to maintaining peace and good order between one another and between themselves and newcomers, and to contributing to the provision of justice (Henderson, 1997).

Many Indigenous people understand treaties as a means of bringing settlers into existing kinship relations, and to teach them about their responsibilities as newcomers to this land.[32] Importantly, these intentions were not frozen in time; if conflicts or issues should arise throughout the course of co-existing in shared spaces, treaties were meant to provide a framework to which future generations could turn.

Let us be clear that we are not implying that people in the prairies can simply turn to treaty to remedy the myriad issues surrounding the Indigenous-settler relationship discussed throughout this book. Indeed, there is no *easy* or *straightforward* solution to issues that are now several centuries in the making and have become well-sedimented in these spaces. In fact, we are of the view that treaties cannot be implemented as they were intended by Indigenous people within, or without dismantling, the current settler colonial structure. However, as our traditional diplomatic practices for negotiating and maintaining relationships across difference, we do believe that they provide important sources of inspiration for alternate ways of interpreting, understanding, and responding to the many inter-societal and political tensions that remain alive in the prairies.

Treaties, at a basic level, are mechanisms for talking to strangers and bringing them into relationship with us. It is no small feat to be able to dialogue and negotiate forms of relationship across linguistic, cultural, political, juridical, economic and spiritual differences. It's even harder to do this when the other party poses (or is perceived to pose) a threat to the other.[33] In negotiating treaty relations, Indigenous leaders already saw the damage that was being caused by newcomer presence; they saw the impact on their traditional way of life and to their animal and human kin, who were succumbing to illness and death. Nevertheless, they sought to enter into negotiations in good faith in the interest of cultivating a better relationship for future generations to inhabit. These negotiations required humility, trust, risk and sacrifice. They required parties, to employ the words of Treaty 6 Elder Peter Waskahat, to undertake a willingness to "meet each other halfway" (1997).[34] No part of this is easy. And neither is the process of activating treaty in our relationships today.

Treaty is work; it takes labour to be in relation with other people, and to hold them accountable to a community or communities. Brenda Macdougall writes about the Cree concept of "wahkootowin" that it is an ongoing political project invested in "linking people and communities in a large, complex web of relationships," but one that is also attuned to the myriad, complex, and messy ways we live—or attempt to live—together (2006, 8).[35]

Further, treaty, in all its messiness and complexity, allows for a relationship that is not predetermined or fixed; rather, it is active, something that must be restored and worked on at different times and in different spaces. Daniel Heath Justice asserts that relationality "is a messy thing. It's about what happens when bodies and imaginations come together in relationship, when boundaries are breached and something else comes into being, for good or ill—or, sometimes, for both" (2018, 104).

Even after treaties have, for the most part, been mis-inhabited and misunderstood by settlers, we have refused to discard our treaties on account of how challenging it has been to implement them. Treaties are by nature meant to be revisited and renewed, which also does not happen seamlessly. Mending or remaking ruptured relations is a complicated and laborious process, just as maintaining existing relations is hard work.

And importantly, treaties are not static. If the modes of relationship that we currently have at our disposal are ill-equipped to allow us to affirm these entangled relations, then perhaps we need to reimagine them, which in turn requires us to contend with the possibility that this might not be possible in the world as it is currently constructed.

To put it simply, in order for there to be good treaty or kinship relations, the world as it is currently constructed, which is to say through the edifices of settler colonialism, need not only to change, but to be dismantled and eradicated. Indeed, this may require engaging with a specifically settler colonial manifestation of what Robin DiAngelo terms "white fragility," in which any challenge to presumed white/colonial entitlements triggers significant stress and defensiveness (55, cited in Hunt 2018).

None of this is to say that we should invest in superficial engagements with treaty that too easily declare that 'we are all treaty people' (Epp, 2008), but rather to recognize the messy, interpersonal work we need to do in order to live together in a good way on these lands. Participating in this work in an ethical way means to recognize that in order for us "all to be treaty people" (if such a thing is possible anymore), then we need to radically restructure or dismantle things as they currently operate—to be more specific, we need to address how settler colonialism currently functions and structures relations between Indigenous and non-Indigenous peoples.

Returning to the narratives of settlement discussed throughout this book, what happens when we contrast the hard work involved in working on our treaty relations with the emphasis placed on individual labour and industriousness that was repeatedly invoked throughout the Stanley trial? What if, instead of privileging the sorts of hard work required to develop land and accumulate capital, we placed a higher importance on the type of hard work involved in talking to strangers and providing them with assistance, even if you perceive them to represent a threat?

Much was made in the trial of the fact that Stanley's actions were undertaken during what the defense described as a "fear-filled, high-energy roller coaster ride" *(R v. Stanley* 2018, 852). In fact, in assessing the manslaughter charge, the jury was asked to determine whether his conduct with the gun was a marked departure from the level of care that "a reasonable person" would have exercised in "the same circumstances." This is important, as Stanley's conduct with the gun undoubtedly did not reflect the level of care that one would normally be expected to exercise "without lawful excuse." How then was he not charged with manslaughter on account of careless use of the gun?

The fact that the situation had escalated quickly was part of what the court saw as necessary context surrounding Stanley's actions. The jury was not asked whether Stanley's use of the gun was reasonable in general, they were asked if it was reasonable in light of "the circumstances," and if his carelessness could be justified through "a lawful excuse" (*R. v. Stanley* 2018, 898). While the court explained to the jury that the concepts of "careless use" and "lawful excuse" are intertwined, they did not include clarification surrounding what "a lawful excuse" would constitute, leaving that very important definition open to the jury's discretion.

To be clear, "the circumstances" described by the defense involve a context wherein the hard-working Stanleys are said to have faced "intruders" (i.e. Indigenous youth) whose presence and behaviours are said to have incited "pure terror" in Gerald Stanley. (*R. v. Stanley* 2018, 848) Yet no one pointed out the ways in which he and Sheldon Stanley's antagonistic response to the youth *as they were attempting to drive off the property* contributed to the 'escalating situation.' Ultimately, these circumstances, which Stanley contributed to, would be used by the defense to argue that Stanley should be found not guilty of manslaughter by committing the unlawful act of careless use of a firearm.

The fear and panic that Stanley claimed to have experienced was a constant, and uninterrogated part of the narrative that dominated the trial.[36] Contrast this with the absolute lack of consideration given to the fear that the Indigenous youth must have experienced after having their windshield smashed in by Sheldon Stanley, after being the target of Gerald Stanley's "warning shots," and ultimately, after some of them saw their friend killed in front of them. The narrative that dominated the trial depended upon the assumption that the youth were antagonists that had to be removed from the property in the interest of the Stanleys' safety, which in turn eclipsed the multiplicity of alternative ways that Gerald Stanley could have engaged with them that day.

The narrative developed by the defense was that when the youths' vehicle entered the yard, they initiated a "roller coaster ride" for Gerald Stanley. After one of the youth sat on a quad, Sheldon Stanley ran to their vehicle and smashed the windshield with a hammer, which is said to have accelerated the "ride." At one point, the defense argued that Sheldon Stanley's decision to smash the windshield was a "measured response," compared to if he had "hit somebody in the face with a—a hammer because they're stealing" *(R v. Stanley,* 842). Having had their windshield smashed, the youth's vehicle veered into one of the Stanley's vehicles, at which point Stanley's anxiety arose from his inability to pinpoint the location of his wife, which led him to retrieve his gun and fire warning shots into the air. The defense argued, "is it unreasonable to fire warning shots when the intruders have tried to […] from Gerry's perspective, intentionally—almost run over your wife […] is it reasonable to attempt to deal with the circumstance to defend you and your family?" *(R. v. Stanley* 2018, 607). And while the defense repeatedly framed Stanley as a man who was simply trying to protect his family, there was no evidence suggesting Stanley acted out of concern for his son or wife; his word was simply taken at face value.[37]

Although there was an absence of critical examination of the Stanleys' behaviours—that is, their violent responses to the presence of the youth—criticism of the presumed behaviour and intentions of the youth was a central part of the defense's narrative.

Stanley was presumed innocent until proven guilty in the courtroom and in the public eye, whereas, from the outset, Colten and his friends were framed as responsible for the

GINA STARBLANKET & DALLAS HUNT

eventual encounter that resulted in his death. Their supposed guilt and complicity in theft was implicit in the stories told both in and outside of the courtroom, and the accompanying narratives all worked to bolster these affective associations and ground them in a context that in many ways predetermines Indigenous peoples as always-already criminals, a sentiment rooted in historical, regional prejudices, and of which the jury would have been aware or susceptible to.

In the Stanley trial, the defense went to great lengths to provide what they saw as "the necessary context" to the story of the day of Colten's death, especially by way of gesturing or allusions. An illustrative example is when Stanley's defense lawyer Spencer tried to have an unrelated liquor store theft—*which occurred 40 miles away from the Stanley farm* in the early morning of Colten's death—admitted into evidence. When Judge Martel Popescul questioned the relevance and value of admitting this liquor store theft, since there was no evidence that Colten or the youth were involved, Spencer suggested that it would help "tell the whole story so the jury knows what happened [...] that's my belief is that ...it's relevant because it's part of the story of that day...it's the start of the misadventure" (*R. v. Stanley* 2018, 649-651, 654).

The court did not allow the inventory of the liquor that was stolen into evidence, but this didn't stop the defense from implying that the youth had been responsible for it. Consider the following exchange between Spencer and one of the youth, Eric Meechance:

Q: Okay. Did you do any break and enters the night before?

A: What?

Q: Did you do a break and enter the night before?

A: No. I was at my grandma's.

Q: Okay. Robbed a liquor store?

A: No. I was at my grandma's (*R. v. Stanley* 2018, 318).

Spencer didn't need the liquor theft to be admitted into evidence or—if it had been admitted—ever show evidence that Colten or the other Indigenous youth were involved in the liquor store robbery for this unrelated event to impact the jury. This is because the associations between Indigeneity, drinking, and troublemaking are very deeply embedded in the psyche of rural prairie settlers.

Not once did the Crown point out the normative nature of rural drinking and driving, among Indigenous and non-Indigenous people alike, in the face of the defense's repeated efforts to represent the Indigenous youth as drunks and troublemakers. Nor did the Crown even attempt to mention that such representations problematically rely on and echo the same logics of Indigenous deviancy, primitiveness, and criminality that informed the prohibition, vagrancy and truancy laws designed to keep Indigenous people out of 'white spaces' from 1884 to 1985 (Stonechild and Waiser 1997).

And no one questioned the fact that the police did not ask Stanley to take a breathalyzer that day to test to see if he could have been drinking. In stark contrast, the RCMP thought it important to smell the breath of Debbie Baptiste—Colten's mother—when telling her of her son's death.

Now, let's contrast the move to frame an unrelated liquor store robbery as part of the "necessary context" surrounding Colten's death, with the absolute lack of what Indigenous people understand to be vital context surrounding Indigenous-settler interactions in Treaty 6 territory.

Not once were treaties mentioned in the trial proceedings by either the Crown or the defense.

To be clear, if the provision of justice in Saskatchewan was carried out in accordance with a treaty frame, Indigenous people would have a more significant role in the structure and implementation of justice systems. Each of the numbered treaties contains an iteration of a commitment from Indigenous peoples to maintain "peace and order" between themselves and between Indigenous and settler people. Many have argued that the peace and order clause both affirms the inherent power and ongoing jurisdiction of treaty Chiefs in the administration of law and governance, while also imposing limitations on the authority of the Crown.[38]

Indigenous jurisdiction in areas of law and governance represent a vital, even if largely unrecognized dimension of treaty implementation. Indeed, Shalene Jobin has argued that Cree epistemologies and legal traditions could inform a far broader conception of justice than the measures of justice available under Canadian law, as they are fundamentally relational and account for the harm committed not just against a victim, but against the many relations that a person constitutes and is constituted by.[39] As Canadian law has incrementally assumed greater primacy over Indigenous peoples since the signing of treaty, so too have individualistic, private property-oriented conceptions of law become privileged over Indigenous legal traditions.

And even within the strictly Euro-Canadian system of 'justice' in which the Stanley case was tried, we can imagine what considerations might have figured more prominently if Treaty 6 was a stronger frame of reference, or if *any other mode of relating*, rather than the polarizing ones embedded in settler colonial narratives of life on the prairies, were brought into the picture. If this were the case, perhaps the incredibly hard work of carrying out non-violent relations would have represented a more important imperative; and, perhaps greater doubt would have been cast on the defense's argument that Indigenous presence, particularly Indigenous presence in a situation where the settler is not in complete control, is enough to incite a level of "terror" necessitating violence. Finally, if treaty was the frame of reference, or even if settler narratives of life on the prairies were critically deconstructed to a greater degree, perhaps violence against Indigenous bodies in these spaces would not have been interpreted as "reasonable."

In many ways, what the Stanley trial illustrates is who gets to be rational in what geographies, and what happens when one transgresses the idea or ideal of settler reason, of settler rationality.

# *Where to From Here?*

Where is the end? Is there even an end? There's probably not, so maybe the best is for us to just keep on going...

—Debbie Baptiste (personal communication)

Rather than analyze the legal proceedings surrounding Colten Boushie's death in great detail throughout this book, we have instead chosen to engage with the politics of which stories were heard and which were ignored during the trial. While the legalities of the trial certainly merit further scrutiny, this was not our purpose; partly because we're not legal scholars, but also because we are centrally concerned with the unheard, the masked, the invisible, the denied but the nevertheless present elements that were at play in and around the Stanley case.

A narrative can be told with gestures, misdirection, and allusions, like a magician's performance. Just as important is the explicit denial of other narratives being told. Narratives that are denied from being enunciated or articulated. Our task in this book was to unravel colonial narratives, and to "story" the often silenced, elided, or effaced histories of ongoing colonial violence.

Taken together, the asymmetries of whose narratives 'count', and the narratives about Indigenous people through which these asymmetries are justified, continue to powerfully shape life (and death) in the prairies. In focusing on settler stories throughout this analysis, we don't intend to offer them greater validity or legitimacy than they deserve. On the contrary, we address these stories in order to deconstruct their presumed neutrality and trace how they were crafted to serve a particular political purpose; mainly, the shoring up of territory claims, the establishment of settler society in prairie spaces, and the concomitant erasure of Indigenous people.

We explore them in order to deconstruct the all too pervasive narratives and stories that are constantly heard and legitimized but not taken as evidence of the continuity of settler colonialism or systemic racism.

This book is an act of re-storying as well, a refusal of the dominant ways Indigenous peoples are understood and consumed, and of the dominant ways that our stories are told within settler narratives. Narratives of Indigeneity are often told within heavily circumscribed parameters: as stories of criminality, narratives of deficiency, and/or overdetermined and overwhelming instances of pathology or trauma. In refusing these settler narratives, we also resist the frames of palatable Indigeneity that are often times requested or, more precisely, demanded of us by settler audiences. Instead, we re-story the narratives that underpin the case of Colten's killing on our own terms, complete with all of its colonial connections and complexities. In doing so, we offer what Mohawk scholar Audra Simpson might dub a "resurgent histor[y]" of Indigeneity in the face of settler colonialism and the histories it narrates (2014, 107).

And yet, there is so much that we cannot capture or articulate, or that we refuse to. While this book deals with violent acts perpetrated against Indigenous youth, we also want to foreground the incredible courage of the Boushie and Baptiste families in the wake of indescribable tragedy. We want to foreground the activist, on-the-ground work of Colten's relatives, and the continual, dogged advocacy they do for and with their relations. We want to foreground that Indigenous peoples, while undoubtedly affected by the processes of settler colonialism, are not passive in the throes of history—that we are active agents carving out pockets of livability in a system that demands and facilitates our deaths. And finally, we want to foreground that Indigenous youth went swimming and felt joy in their ancestral territories one day, that they asserted their presence on lands

GINA STARBLANKET & DALLAS HUNT

that have been a part of them since before they were born, and that, acting as an agent of history, as the culmination of centuries of settler colonial rage and entitlement, Gerald Stanley, and eventually his supporters, worked and have continued to work to stifle that joy.

We refuse to let them.

# Bibliography

Andersen, Chris. 2014. *Métis: Race, Recognition, and the Struggle for Indigenous Peoplehood*. Vancouver: UBC Press.

Asaka, Ikuko. 2017. *Tropical Freedom: Climate, Settler Colonialism, and Black Exclusion in the Age of Emancipation*. Duke University Press.

Asch, Michael. 2014. *On Being Here To Stay: Treaties and Aboriginal Rights in Canada*. Toronto: University of Toronto Press.

Arneil, Barbara. 1996. *John Locke and America*. Don Mills: Oxford University Press.

Backhouse, Constance. 1999. *Colour-Coded: A Legal History of Racism in Canada, 1900-1950*. Toronto: University of Toronto Press.

Barker, Joanne. 2018. "The Empire's Terrorist: Indigeneity and the State" paper presented at the American Studies Association Annual Meeting, Atlanta, GA.

Belmessous, Saliha. 2014. *Empire by Treaty: Negotiating European Expansion, 1600-1900*. Don Mills: Oxford University Press.

Belshaw, John Douglas. 2016. *Canadian History: Post-Confederation.* Available online at: <https://opentextbc.ca/postconfederation/chapter/5-2-immigration-and-the-national-policy/>. Open Textbook.

Borrows, John. 2010. *Canada's Indigenous Constitution*. Toronto: University of Toronto Press.

Borrows, John. 2017. "Indigenous Constitutionalism: Pre-Existing Legal Genealogies in Canada," in *The Oxford Handbook of the Canadian Constitution*, edited by Peter Oliver, Patrick Macklem, and Nathalie Des Rosiers. Oxford: Oxford University Press, 31.

Brunyeel, Kevin. 2017. "Creolizing Collective Memory: Refusing the Settler Memory of the Reconstruction Era." *Journal of French and Francophone Philosophy 25*: 36-44.

Campbell Scott, Duncan. 1906. *The Last of the Indian Treaties* (Vol. 40). Scribners.

Cardinal, Harold, and Walter Hildebrand. 2000. *Treaty Elders of Saskatchewan: Our Dream is that Our Peoples Will One Day be Clearly Recognized as Nations.* Calgary: University of Calgary Press.

Carter, Sarah. 2016. *Imperial Plots: Women, Land, and the Spadework of British Colonialism on the Canadian Prairies.* Winnipeg: University of Manitoba Press.

Casid, Jill. 2005. *Sowing Empire: Landscape and Colonization.* Minneapolis: University of Minnesota Press.

CBC News. 2017 "'I've seen no evidence that race played any part': Gerald Stanley's lawyer comments on the Colten Boushie case". *CBC News' Out in the Open*, January 6, 2017. https://www.cbc.ca/radio/outintheopen/what-does-colten-boushie-say-about-us-1.4039219/i-ve-seen-no-evidence-that-race-played-any-part-gerald-stanley-s-lawyer-comments-on-the-colten-boushie-case-1.3923957.

Chandler, Graham. 2016. "Selling the Prairie Good Life." *Canada's History.* Accessed February 2, 2020.https://www.canadashistory.ca/explore/settlement-immigration/selling-the-prairie-good-life.

Conway, John. 2014. *The Rise of the New West: The History of a Region in Confederation.* Toronto: James Lorimer & Company Ltd., Publishers.

Cottrell, Michael. "The Irish in Saskatchewan, 1850-1930: a study of intergenerational ethnicity." In *Prairie Forum*, vol. 24, pp. 185-209. 1999.

Coulthard, Glen. 2014. *Red Skin, White Masks: Rejecting the Colonial Politics of Recognition.* Minneapolis: University of Minnesota Press.

Cruikshank, Julie. 2003. "Discovery of Gold on the Klondike: Perspectives from Oral Tradition". In *Reading Beyond Words: Contexts for Native History* (Second Edition), edited by Jennifer S.H. Brown and Elizabeth Vibert, 433-453. Toronto: University of Toronto Press.

CJME News. "FSIN blasts RCMP over release about shooting". *CJME News,* August 12, 2016. https://www.cjme.com/2016/08/12/ fsin-blasts-rcmp-over-release-about-shooting/.

Crosby, Andrew and Jeffrey Monaghan. 2018. *Policing Indigenous Movements: Dissent and the Security State.* Halifax: Fernwood Publishing.

Dafnos, Tia, Scott Thompson, and Martin French. 2016. "Surveillance and the Colonial Dream: Canada's Surveillance of Indigenous Protest". In *National Security, Surveillance, and Emergencies: Canadian and Australian Sovereignty Compared,* edited by Randy K. Lippert, Kevin Walby, Ian Warren, and Darren Palmer, 319-342. Basingstoke: Palgrave MacMillan.

Dafnos, Tia. 2019. "The Enduring Settler-Colonial Emergency: Indian Affairs and Contemporary Emergency Management in Canada". *Settler Colonial Studies* 9(3): 379-395.

Daschuk, James William. 2013. *Clearing the Plains: Disease, Politics of Starvation, and the Loss of Aboriginal Life.* Regina: University of Regina Press.

Dhillon, Jaskiran and Will Parish. 2019. "Indigenous people outraged at Canada police's possible use of lethal force". *The Guardian,* December 24, 2019. https://www.theguardian.com/world/2019/dec/24/ indigenous-people-outraged-at-canada-polices-possible-use-of-lethal-force.

Day, Iyko. *Alien Capital: Asian Racialization and the Logic of Settler Colonial Capitalism.* Duke University Press, 2016.

Edgar, Alistair, Rupinder Mangat, and Bessma Momani, eds. 2020. *Strengthening the Canadian Armed Forces through Diversity and Inclusion.* Toronto: University of Toronto Press.

Environics Institute. (2016) Canadian Public Opinion on Aboriginal Peoples: Final Report. Toronto. https://tidescanada.org/wp-content/uploads/2016/06/ Canadian-Public-Opinion-on-Aboriginal-Peoples-2016-FINAL-REPORT.pdf.

Erickson, Lesley. 2011. *Westward Bound: Sex, Violence, the Law, and the Making of a Settler Society.* Vancouver: UBC Press.

Friesen, Gerald., 1987. *The Canadian Prairies: A History.* Toronto: University of Toronto Press.

Ford, Lisa. 2011. *Settler Sovereignty: Jurisdiction and Indigenous People in America and Australia, 1788-1836*. Cambridge: Harvard University Press.

Gaudry, Adam. 2013. The Métis-ization of Canada: The Process of Claiming Louis Riel, Métissage, and the Métis People as Canada's Mythical Origin. A*boriginal Policy Studies*, *2*(2).

Green, Joyce. 2017. "Balancing Strategies: Aboriginal Women and Constitutional Rights in Canada". In *Making Space for Indigenous Feminism* (Second Edition), edited by Joyce Green, 36-51. Winnipeg: Fernwood Publishing.

Green, Joyce. 2006. "From Stonechild to Social Cohesion: Anti-Racist Challenges for Saskatchewan." *Canadian Journal of Political Science* Vol.39 (3), 2006.

Green, Joyce. 1995. Towards a Détente With History: Confronting Canada's Colonial Legacy. *International Journal of Canadian Studies* 12, Fall.

Harring, Sidney L. 1998. *White Man's Law: Native People in Nineteenth-Century Canadian Jurisprudence*. Toronto: University of Toronto Press.

Henderson, James Youngblood. 2000. The Context of the State of Nature. In *Reclaiming Indigenous Voice and Vision*, edited by Marie Battiste. Vancouver: University of British Columbia Press. pp.11-38.

Henderson, James Youngblood. 1997. "Interpreting Sui Generis Treaties" 36 Alta L Rev 46 at 82.

Hunt, Dallas. 2018. "'In search of our better selves': Totem Transfer Narratives and Indigenous Futurities." *American Indian Culture and Research Journal* 42.1: 71-90.

Iacobucci, Frank. 2013. *First Nations Representation on Ontario Juries.* https://www.attorneygeneral.jus.gov.on.ca/english/about/pubs/iacobucci/First_Nations_Representation_Ontario_Juries.html.

Justice, Daniel Heath. 2018. *Why Indigenous Literatures Matter*. Waterloo: Wilfrid Laurier University Press.

Kauanui, J. Kēhaulani and Patrick Wolfe. 2012. "Settler Colonialism Then and Now". *Politica & Societa* 2: 235-258.

LaRocque, Emma. *When the Other is Me: Native Resistance Discourse, 1850–1990*. Winnipeg: U of Manitoba P, 2010.

Levasseur, Joanne. "People on the Prairies Less Tolerant, CBC Poll Says" *CBC News* November 2014. https://www.cbc.ca/news/canada/manitoba/people-on-the-prairies-less-tolerant-cbc-poll-says-1.2831876.

Macdougall, Brenda. 2012. "The Myth of Métis Cultural Ambivalence" in *Contours of a People: Métis, Family, Mobility, and History*, edited by Nicole St-Onge, Carolyn Podruchny, and Brenda Macdougall, 422.

Macdougall, Brenda. 2011. *One of the Family: Metis Culture in Nineteenth-Century Northwestern Saskatchewan*. Vancouver: UBC Press.

Martens, Kathleen and Trina Roache. 2018. "RCMP Facebook group claims Colten Boushie 'got what he deserved'". *APTN News*, February 15. https://aptnnews.ca/2018/02/15/rcmp-facebook-group-claims-colten-boushie-got-deserved/.

McHugh Paul, and Lisa Ford. 2012. "Settler Sovereignty and the Shapeshifting Crown". In *Between Indigenous and Settler Governance*, edited by Lisa Ford and Tim Rowse, 35-46. New York: Routledge.

Monture-Angus, Patricia A. 1996. "Lessons in Decolonization: Aboriginal Overrepresentation in Canadian Criminal Justice". In *Visions of the Heart: Canadian Aboriginal Issues*, edited by David Long and Olive Dickason, 335-354. Don Mills: Oxford University Press.

Moreton-Robinson, Aileen. 2015. *The White Possessive: Property, Power, and Indigenous Sovereignty*. Minneapolis: University of Minnesota Press.

Morris, Alexander. 1880. *The Treaties of Canada with the Indians of Manitoba and the North-West Territories: Including the Negotiations on which they were Based, and Other Information relating thereto*. Belfords: Clarke.

Opekokew, Delia, 1992. "The Nature and Status of the Oral Promises in Relation to the Written Terms of the Treaties," Public Policy and Aboriginal Peoples, 1965-1992, no. 192, p.21, INAC Library, E92 R702.

Rifkin, Mark. *Settler Common Sense: Queerness and Everyday Colonialism in the American Renaissance*. U of Minnesota Press, 2014.

Roach, Kent. 2019. *Canadian Justice, Indigenous Justice: The Gerald Stanley and Colten Boushie Case*. Montreal-Kingston: McGill-Queen's University Press.

Rotz, Sarah. 2017. "'They Took Our Beads, It Was a Fair Trade, Get Over It': Settler Colonial Logics, Racial Hierarchies and Material Dominance in Canadian Agriculture". *Geoforum* 82: 158-169.

Royal Commission on Aboriginal Peoples. 1996. *Bridging the Cultural Divide: A Report on Aboriginal People and Criminal Justice in Canada*. Ottawa: Minister of Supply and Services Canada.

Palmer, Howard. 1992. "Strangers and Stereotypes: The Rise of Nativism, 1880-1920". In *The Prairie West: Historical Readings*, edited by R. Douglas Francis and Howard Palmer, 308-334. Edmonton: University of Alberta Press.

Pasternak, Shiri and Tia Dafnos. 2018. "How Does a Settler State Secure the Circuitry of Capital?" *Environment and Planning D: Society and Space* 36(4): 739-757.

Perry, Adele. 1997. "'Fair Ones of a Purer Caste': White Women and Colonialism in Nineteenth-Century British Columbia". *Feminist Studies* 23(3): 501-524.

Pitsula, James M. 2013. *Keeping Canada British: The Ku Klux Klan in 1920s Saskatchewan*. UBC Press.

Satzewich, Vic and Terry Wotherspoon. 2000. *First Nations: Race, Class and Gender Relations*, vol. 6. Regina: University of Regina Press, 18-28.

Saul, John Ralston. 2008. *A Fair Country: Telling Truths About Canada*. Toronto: Penguin Canada.

Shantz, Jacob. 1874. *Province of Manitoba: Information for Intending Emigrants*. Ottawa: Department of Agriculture.

Sharpe, Christina. 2016. *In the Wake: On Blackness and Being*. Duke University Press.

Simpson, Audra. 2014. *Mohawk Interruptus: Political Life across the Borders of Settler States*. Durham: Duke University Press.

Simpson, Audra. 2016. The State is a Man: Theresa Spence, Loretta Saunders and the Gender of Settler Sovereignty. *Theory & Event*, *19*(4).

Simpson, Leanne Betasamosake. 2008. "Looking after Gdoo-naaganinaa: Precolonial Nishnaabeg Diplomatic and Treaty Relationships". *Wicazo Sa Review* 23(2): 29-42.

Simpson, Leanne Betasamosake. 2017. *As We Have Always Done: Indigenous Freedom through Radical Resistance*. Minneapolis: University of Minnesota Press.

Singh, Jakeet. 2004. "Re-articulating multiculturalism: Transcending the Difference-Blind Liberal Approach". In *Racism, Eh?* edited by Camille A. Nelson and Charmaine A. Nelson, 444-455. Concord: Captus Press.

St. Germain, Jill. 2001. *Indian Treaty-Making Policy in the United States and Canada, 1867-1877*. Toronto: University of Toronto Press.

Starblanket, Gina. 2019. "The Numbered Treaties and the Politics of Incoherency" *Canadian Journal of Political Science* 52(3): 443-459.

Starblanket, Gina. 2019. "Constitutionalizing (In) justice: Treaty Interpretation and the Containment of Indigenous Governance." *Constitutional Forum* 28(13).

Stark, Heidi. 2010. "Respect, Responsibility, and Renewal: The Foundations of Anishinaabe Treaty-Making with the United States and Canada". *American Indian Culture and Research Journal* 34(2): 145-164.

Stark, Heidi. 2012. "Marked by Fire: Anishinaabe Articulations of Nationhood in Treaty-Making with the United States and Canada". *American Indian Quarterly* 36(2): 119-149.

Stark, Heidi. 2016. "Criminal Empire: The Making of the Savage in a Lawless Land". *Theory & Event* 19(4).

Stonechild, Blair and Bill Waiser. 1997. *Loyal Till Death: Indians and the North-West Rebellion*. Calgary: Fifth House.

Tait, Myra J. and Kiera Ladner. 2018. "Economic Development through Treaty Reparations in New Zealand and Canada". *Canadian Journal of Law and Society* 33(1): 61-83.

Taylor, John Leonard. 1985. *Treaty research report: Treaty six (1876)*. Treaties and Historical Research Centre, Indian and Northern Affairs Canada.

*The Free Library*. S.v. Saskatoon police chief admits starlight cruises are not new.." Retrieved Feb 03 2020 from https://www.thefreelibrary.com/Saskatoon+police+chief+admits+starlight+cruises+are+not+new.-a0105369747.

Thobani, Sunera. 2007. *Exalted Subjects: Studies in the Making of Race and Nation in Canada*. Toronto: University of Toronto Press.

Tully, James. 1995. *Strange Multiplicity: Constitutionalism in an Age of Diversity*. PLACE: Cambridge University Press.

Veracini, Lorenzo. 2010. *Settler Colonialism: A Theoretical Overview*. Basingstoke: Palgrave Macmillan.

Young, Robert. 2001. *Postcolonialism: An Historical Introduction*. Oxford: Blackwell.

Walker, James Barr. 1881. *Experiences of Pioneer Life in the Early Settlements and Cities of the West*. Chicago: Sumner & Co.

Waskahat, Peter (Frog Lake First Nation, Treaty 6). November 12, 1997, Treaty Elders Forum, Jackfish Lake Lodge, Cochin, Saskatchewan.

Wilderson III, Frank B. *Red, White & Black: Cinema and the Structure of US Antagonisms*. Duke University Press, 2010.

Williams, Robert. 1997. *Linking Arms Together: American Indian Treaty Visions of Law and Peace, 1600-1800*. Don Mills: Oxford University Press.

Wolfe, Patrick. 2006. "Settler Colonialism and the Elimination of the Native". *Journal of Genocide Research* 8(4): 387-409.

Wolfe, Patrick. 2016. *Traces of History: Elementary Structures of Race*. New York: Verso Books.

Wynter, Sylvia. "Unsettling the Coloniality of Being/Power/Truth/Freedom: Towards the Human, After Man, its Overrepresentation—An Argument." *CR: The new centennial review* 3, no. 3 (2003): 257-337.

Zakreski, Dan. 2017. "Iain Stables given conditional sentence for stealing $1.2M in farm equipment". *CBC News*, December 15. https://www.cbc.ca/news/canada/saskatoon/iain-stables-conditional-sentence-farm-equipment-1.4450845.

## *Legal Cases:*

R. v. Barton, 2019, SCC 33.

R. v. Stanley, 2017, E-File 2017-04-03OCPStanleyG (Preliminary Inquiry)

R. v. Stanley, 2018, E-File 2018-01-29OCQStanleyG

# *Endnotes*

1    Throughout this book, we refer to Colten Boushie as "Colten" as much
     as possible in an intentional effort to foreground his humanity. We never
     met Colten, but we use his first name because this is how the family has
     spoken about him in the conversations we have had.

2    Gerald Stanley's defense attorney would go on to the argue that the
     execution-style killing was the result of a "hang-fire," which is when
     there is a short delay between the pulling of a trigger and when a bullet is
     released from the barrel of the gun. The defense attempted to introduce
     anecdotal evidence from reddit.com to bolster their claim of a hang-fire
     but were overruled by the court. The hang-fire defense was not proven,
     and in fact was contradicted by the testimony of firearm experts. Yet
     Gerald Stanley walks free, in no small part owing to the narrative of "self-
     defence" that was carefully crafted (but not explicitly asserted) and which
     framed the hang-fire defence. For the purposes of this book, the stories
     that structure the 'unspoken' narrative of self-defence are what we are
     interested in.

3    https://nationalpost.com/news/canada/gerald-stanleys-magical-gun-the-
     extremely-unlikely-defence-that-secured-his-acquittal

4    The words "reasonable" and "reason" were used throughout the trial in
     reference to Stanley's actions.

5    Under Canadian law, $2^{nd}$ degree murder generally involves intentionally
     causing the death of another person, or intentionally causing bodily harm
     that is likely to cause death. Manslaughter refers to killing without intent.
     In Gerald Stanley's case, he was charged with $2^{nd}$ degree murder and if
     the jury were to find that he lacked the intention to fire his weapon at
     the occupants of the vehicle, they were to move to the lesser charge of
     manslaughter. In deciding whether he was guilty of manslaughter, the jury
     was asked to focus on the question of whether Stanley used the firearm in
     a careless manner. Careless use of a firearm involves conduct that shows
     a marked departure from the standard of care that a reasonable person
     would exercise in similar circumstances. Thus, the jury was tasked with
     assessing the reasonableness of Stanley's actions in light of the context.

6   It read "...five individuals entered onto private property by vehicle in the
    rural area and were confronted by property owners who were outside and
    witnessed their arrival. The occupants of the vehicle were not known to
    the property owners...one adult male (who arrived in the vehicle) was
    suffering from an apparent gunshot wound and was declared deceased
    at the scene...Three occupants from the vehicle, including two females
    (one being a youth) and one adult male were taken into custody as
    part of a related theft investigation." ("FSIN blasts RCMP over release
    about shooting" CJME News, August 12, 2016. https://www.cjme.
    com/2016/08/12/fsin-blasts-rcmp-over-release-about-shooting/).

7   Treaty 4 was signed in 1874 and encompasses most of Southern
    Saskatchewan and portions of Alberta and Manitoba, while Treaty 8 was
    signed in 1899 and encompasses northern Alberta, parts of northeast
    British Columbia and northwest Saskatchewan as well as parts of
    southern Northwest Territories. While we have experienced the impacts
    of colonialism within our lives and relationships with our families and
    communities, we also recognize that neither of us have had the same
    experiences of racialization as someone who is visibly Indigenous on
    the prairies, an issue we think is important to foreground given how
    racialization played out in the events preceding, during, and succeeding
    the Stanley trial.

8   For just one example of such "hybridity," see John Raulston Saul's
    (2008) characterization of the Canadian nation itself as "Métis," a move
    that draws on the identity of a distinct political community to symbolize
    the purportedly harmonious fusion of Indigenous and European bodies
    that Canada lays claim to. For important critiques of this approach, see
    Anderson, 2014; Gaudry, 2013; MacDougall 2012.

9   See Leanne Simpson, 2017; Audra Simpson, 2016.

10  See, for instance, Ryan Eyford, *White Settler Reserve: New Iceland and
    the Colonization of the Canadian West* Vancouver, UBC Press (2016).

11  For a separate analysis of the notion of settler "common sense" see Rifkin
    (2014).

12  See, for instance: Belmessous, 2014; Kelley, 2017; Veracini, 2010;
    Wolfe, 2006, 2016; Young, 2001.

13    For some foundational theorizations of this, see Coulthard, 2014;
      Moreton-Robinson, 2015; A. Simpson, 2014; L. Simpson, 2017; Wolfe,
      2006.

14    See, among others, Asch, 2014; St. Germain, 2001and 2008;
      Starblanket, 2019; Stark, 2010 and 2012; Simpson, 2008; Williams,
      1997.

15    While treaty land entitlement processes are meant to provide redress
      for enforced dispossession under the treaties, this is an outstanding
      obligation which both federal and provincial governments perpetually fail
      to satisfy. See Ladner and Tait, 2018.

16    See Cottrell, 1999; Pitsula, 2013.

17    See, for instance, Royal Commission on Aboriginal Peoples, *Bridging the
      Cultural Divide: A Report on Aboriginal People and Criminal Justice in
      Canada* (Minister of Supply and Services Canada Ottawa, Canada, 1996);
      Aboriginal Justice Implementation Commission, *Report of the Aboriginal
      Justice Inquiry of Manitoba* (Public Inquiry into the Administration of
      Justice and Aboriginal People, 1991); Frank Iacobucci, *First Nations
      Representation on Ontario Juries: Report of the Independent Review
      Conducted by the Honourable Frank Iacobucci* (Ontario Ministry of
      the Attorney General, 2013); Patricia A Monture-Angus, "Lessons in
      Decolonization: Aboriginal Overrepresentation in Canadian Criminal
      Justice," in David Long & Olive Dickason, eds., *Visions of the Heart:
      Canadian Aboriginal Issues* (Oxford: Oxford University Press, 1996).·

18    Many Indigenous writers and educators, as well as sex workers and sex
      worker advocates, have spoken or written about the murder of Pamela
      George. That said, the most well-known and widely-read piece on the
      murder of Pamela George is most likely Sherene Razack's "Gendered
      Racial Violence and Spatialized Justice: The Murder of Pamela George,"
      in the edited collection *Race, Space, and the Law: Unmapping a White
      Settler Society* (Razack, 2002).

19    For more on the processes of "settler memory," see Kevin Bruyneel,
      2017.

20   Wolfe, Patrick. "Land, Labor, and Difference: Elementary Structures of Race." *The American Historical Review* 106, no. 3 (2001), 866-905.

21   In 1885, the Canadian government introduced the pass system, a policy indicating whether or not Indigenous peoples were "allowed" to leave reserve spaces, a decision often at the discretion of Indian Agents (government bureaucrats who often harboured racist ideas of what spaces Indigenous peoples belonged to or were allowed to exist in). According to James Daschuk, the pass system "was implemented to limit the mobility of treaty Indians, keeping them on their reserves and away from European communities" (161). Further, the imposition of the pass system "undermined access to game and crippled the economic prospects of reserve communities" (161), as well as "curtail[ed] broad participation in Indigenous religious ceremonies" (171).

22   Here we recall how the figure of the Buffalo has been appropriated by Alberta politicians in a "Buffalo Declaration" which demands recognition of Alberta's cultural distinctiveness (see: https://buffalodeclaration.com/). This declaration perversely invokes the Buffalo, which is widely regarded as a symbol of Indigenous political/cultural/social life, to situate Alberta as a neglected 'colony' relative to the rest of Canada. Unsurprisingly, this declaration ignores the existence of the Buffalo Treaty and other Indigenous treaties that exist in these same spaces.

23   To be clear, this contemporary 'threat' that Indigenous people pose to settler economies and livelihoods is the growing recognition, at domestic and international levels, that Indigenous people do indeed hold rights to our ancestral territories and to governance.

24   See also Jodi Byrd, *The Transit of Empire, Minnesota* University of Minnesota (2011).

25   See Dafnos 2019; Dafnos, Thompson, and French 2016; Crosby and Monaghan 2018; Pasternak and Dafnos 2018.

26   See Jaskiran Dhillon and Will Parish (2019), "Indigenous People Outraged at Canada's Possible Use of Lethal Force" *The Guardian,* Accessed online at: https://www.theguardian.com/world/2019/dec/24/indigenous-people-outraged-at-canada-polices-possible-use-of-lethal-force.

**27** See Sarah Hunt, "More than a Poster Campaign: Redefining Colonial Violence," *Decolonization: Indigeneity, Education & Society*: https:// decolonization.wordpress.com/2013/02/14/more-than-a-poster-campaign-redefining-colonial-violence/

**28** For further proof of the differential treatment of Indigenous and non-Indigenous peoples, one only need look to white Saskatchewan cattle rancher Iain Stables. Stables admitted to stealing $1.2 million worth of farm equipment and was sentenced to three years on probation and two years of house arrest (Zakreski 2017). Tellingly, little was made of Stables's crimes or his conviction; no letters were sent to politicians or government officials, no massive media circus that routinely represented Indigenous peoples as "angry," "dangerous," or "unreasonable." Indeed, it was the perceived "reasonableness" that accompanies settler whiteness that allowed Stables the ability to move through the area unnoticed to steal items. Here, a few things should be clear/troubling: the nature of Stables punishment (probation, house arrest) for *verified* theft, as well as the prosecution and defense making a joint submission to the court. In short, Stables was able to stay relatively unremarkable, an aberration as a white settler who committed a significant property crime and yet who was able to keep his life in the process. While he was ordered to undergo a mental health assessment, this was ultimately an exercise in how to excuse a white settler for committing a crime, whereas when a marginalized person is considered "mentally ill," they are often further punished or subjected to violence.

**29** This poll conducted a regional analysis of the data using a statistical method called segmentation analysis in order to establish the opinions of those polled toward Indigenous people

**30** We began to reflect upon "interpretive frames" in a new manner after hearing Leroy Littlebear explain them to us in a workshop at a 2019 Indigenous Knowledge Gathering.

**31** See J.L. Taylor's (1985) research report on Treaty 6, and Cardinal and Hildebrandt's (2000) Treaty Elders of Saskatchewan.

**32** See James Rodger Miller, *Compact, Contract, Covenant: Aboriginal Treaty-Making in Canada* (University of Toronto Press, 2009); Sarah Carter, "Your Great Mother across the Salt Sea: Prairie First Nations, the British Monarchy and the Vice Regal Connection to 1900," *Manitoba History*, no. 48 (2004).

**33** We began to think about these challenges in this way after hearing a public lecture given by Willie Ermine on ethical spaces of engagement at the Southern Alberta Institute of Technology in March 2020.

**34** Specifically, the following words from Elder Peter Waskahat provide important insight into the intended nature of the relationship: "When the Queen's representative came to Fort Edmonton, the Chiefs did not go where the Treaty Commissioner's ships were docked. They met him half way from that location. From where he waited for them they met half way from that point from Fort Edmonton. Why the Chiefs did that was because if they had gone all the way to where the commissioner resided, it would appear that the Chiefs were submitting to every expectation of the Treaty Commissioner's wishes. And so the two sovereigns, the White people, and the Indigenous or Cree people, they met half way, and when they arrived at the location where they were to negotiate Treaty" (Waskahat, 1997).

**35** See any number of Cree dictionaries for more on the concept of, or alternative (though related) definitions for, wahkohtowin. One such example is the *Alberta Elders' Cree Dictionary* (1998) published through the University of Alberta Press. Also, it is worth mentioning that differences abound in the Cree language, not only in terms of different dialects, but also in terms of the differences in orthography and diction within the same dialect. While Macdougall chooses to use two [o]s in her spelling of "wahkootowin," in our own experiences in learning the language, we have encountered different spellings. That said, we are all speaking to the same theoretical and philosophical concepts that underpin a term like wahkohtowin (even if we may spell the term differently).

**36** When asked what he was thinking as he moved towards the youths' vehicle, Gerald Stanley contextualized his fear by citing "a couple murders [that] took place just down the road from us" when he and his family moved in "about 30 years ago" (*R. v. Stanley*, 687-688)

**37**     Stanley claimed to be concerned for his wife because "he could not see her" near the lawn mower. After the shooting, he looked over to the mower and indicated that "Dee was standing there and that he didn't know where she came from." The Crown did not interrogate these inconsistencies, or the credibility of Stanley's recollections at a time when, in his own admission, he "just wasn't thinking straight."

**38**     Henderson, "Interpreting Sui Generis Treaties," *Alta. L. Rev.* 36 (1997), 83. In Saskatchewan, the Federation of Saskatchewan Indian Nations' 1979 document entitled *The Spirit and Intent of Treaty* outlines Indigenous peoples' understanding of the areas of jurisdiction that were retained under the numbered treaties, which include judicial powers such as national law, tribal law, domestic (civil) law, Indian courts, Indian police, corrections, Indian rights, protection, and civil rights. Federation of Saskatchewan Indian Nations, *The Spirit and Intent of Treaties* (1979), 12.

**39**     Shalene Jobin. "Understanding #JusticeforColten Through Indigenous Systems of Knowledge." Lecture given at the University of Calgary on October 12, 2018.

# *Biographies*

**DALLAS HUNT** is Cree and a member of Wapsewsipi (Swan River First Nation) in Treaty 8 territory in Northern Alberta, Canada. He has had creative and critical work published in the Malahat Review, Arc Poetry, Canadian Literature, Settler Colonial Studies, and the American Indian Culture and Research Journal. His first children's book, *Awâsis and the World-Famous Bannock*, was published through Highwater Press and was nominated for the Elizabeth Mrazik-Cleaver Canadian Picture Book Award.

**DR. GINA STARBLANKET** is Canada Research Chair in the Politics of Decolonization and an Assistant Professor in the Department of Political Science at the University of Calgary. Gina is Cree/ Saulteaux and a member of the Star Blanket Cree Nation in Treaty 4 territory. She is co-editor of the 5th edition of *Visions of the Heart: Issues Involving Indigenous People in Canada* and has publications in the *Canadian Journal of Political Science*, the *American Indian Culture and Research Journal*, and *Constitutional Forum*. Her research focuses on Indigenous and Canadian politics, and takes up issues surrounding treaty implementation, gender, Indigenous feminism, decolonization, and Indigenous resurgence.